Born at the Battlefield
of Gettysburg

HARRIETTE C. RINALDI

Markus Wiener Publishers
Princeton

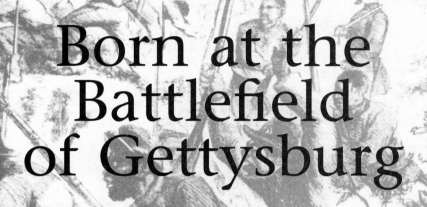

Born at the Battlefield of Gettysburg

An African-American Family Saga

Illustration on p. i: Detail of the back side of "The Spirit of Freedom," the African-American Civil War Memorial at 10th & U Streets, N.W., in Washington, D.C. Sculptor: Ed Hamilton, Louisville, Kentucky. Commissioned by the District of Columbia, 1993. Photo: edhamiltonworks.com

Illustration sources: Camino Books, Philadelphia; Princeton University Library; private collections of the author and publisher.

For information write to:
Markus Wiener Publishers
231 Nassau St., Princeton, NJ 08542
www.markuswiener.com

Book design: Cheryl Mirkin
Cover design: Maria Madonna Davidoff

Library of Congress Cataloging-in-Publication Data
Rinaldi, Harriette C.
    Born at the battlefield of Gettysburg : an African-American family saga/ Harriette C. Rinaldi.
    Includes bibliographical references and index.
    ISBN 1-55876-331-7 (hardcover : alk. paper)
    1. Chambers, Victor, 1863-1943. 2. Chambers, Victor, 1863-1943—Family. 3. African Americans—Biography. 4. Mothers and sons—United States—Biography. 5. Women slaves—Virginia—Biography. 6. Fugitive slaves—United States—Biography. 7. Slaves—United States—Social conditions. 8. Slavery—United States—History. I. Title.
    E185.96.R535 2004
    973'.0496073'0092—dc22
    [B]   2003027400

Paperback ISBN 1-55876-332-5

Markus Wiener Publishers books are printed
in the United States of America on acid-free paper,
and meet the guidelines for permanence and durability
of the committee on production guidelines
for book longevity of the council on library resources

To my parents,

Edward and Harriet Rinaldi

C O N T E N T S

We are people to whom the past is forever speaking. We listen to it because we cannot help ourselves, for the past speaks to us with many voices. Far out of the dark nowhere, which is the time before we were born, men who were flesh of our flesh and bone of our bone, went through fire and storm to break a path to the future. What they did— the lives they lived, the sacrifices they made, the stories they told and the songs they sang and, finally, the deaths they died—make up our own experience. We cannot cut ourselves off from it. It is as real to us as something that happened last week. It is a basic part of our heritage as Americans.

—*Bruce Catton, America Goes to War*

My great-grandfather, Michael R. Carroll, fought on the Union side during the Civil War, where he saw action in many important engagements, including the Battle of Gettysburg. But this is not a story about my great-grandfather. Had he not been at Gettysburg during those hot days in July of 1863, however, this story of Victor D. Chambers and his mother would never have been known. Thanks to letters written by Mr. Chambers to my great-grandfather, the remarkable woman who was Mr. Chambers's mother emerges from her anonymity—while anonymity still enshrouds many thousands of unheralded women who suffered under the scourge of slavery, the legacy of which continued to afflict this country well beyond the end of the Civil War. While neither was aware of the other's presence at the time, both my great-grandfather and Victor Chambers's mother were at Gettysburg in early July 1863. The fortitude and conviction that led her to Gettysburg are as worthy of respectful remembrance as those of the men who fought there. While my great-grandfather's service to his country was recognized publicly, the life of Victor Chambers's mother is not to be found in any news reports, historical accounts, or archives, but rather in the words of her son, as he told

CIVIL WAR VETERAN TREASURES SWORD

Veteran Proud of Sword

Michael R. Carroll Polishing Up Weapon in Preparation for Memorial Day.

A sword presented to Michael R. Carroll, Civil War veteran of this city, when he was commissioned a lieutenant in the Union Army 67 years ago, is today the proudest possession of the veteran, who in his 91st year is again preparing to take part in Memorial Day exercises.

Mr. Carroll has never failed to take part in the observance of Memorial Day and each year carries with him the sword which he has carefully cared for since the completion of his service. Letters of his name engraved on the weapon have been worn almost completely away and the veteran is spending considerable time polishing it so that it will be at a brightest May 30.

A well-known resident of the Fox Point section where he lived for more than 40 years, Mr. Carroll is the father of Harbor Master William H. Carroll. The veteran formerly served as superintendent of the city yards and made his home on Tockwotton street until he was forced to move when his house was in the path of the new Fox Point boulevard two years ago. He now lives at 44 Pitman street.

Born In New York

Mr. Carroll was born in New York City, where he enlisted for service in the Civil War in February, 1862. Enlisting at the age of 21 he saw active service during more than 3½ years of the struggle and after two years of service was made a lieutenant.

In the many battles in which he took part during the war Mr. Carroll had several narrow escapes from fatal injury. During the first struggle in which he engaged he fought beside the first man in his regiment to fall.
A few months after entering the war

Michael R. Carroll of 44 Pitman street is 91. He plans to ride again in the Memorial Day parade this year, carrying the sword which has been his proud possession since he fought in the war between the States.

The Providence Evening Bulletin article of May 13, 1931,
that inspired Victor Chambers to write to the author's great-grandfather

them many years later to my great-grandfather.

The *Providence Evening Bulletin* of Wednesday, May 13, 1931, carried a feature story entitled "A Civil War Veteran Treasures Sword." Under a photograph of my great-grandfather wearing his Civil War uniform, the caption read, "Michael R. Carroll is 91. He plans to ride again in the Memorial Day parade this year, carrying the sword which has been his proud possession since he fought in the war between the

States." The *Evening Bulletin* article noted that the old veteran was born in New York City, enlisted in the Union army in 1862, and was involved in active service for the duration of the Civil War. At Gettysburg, Lieutenant Carroll's unit, the 73rd Infantry under General Daniel Sickles, commander of the Union army's Third Corps, entered the battle with 324 men and 25 officers and finished the three-day battle with only 100 men and 8 officers. The young lieutenant took part in all of his unit's actions during the horrendous battle, including the awesome attack by Confederate General William Barksdale of Mississippi.

A few days after the article appeared, Michael Carroll received a letter from a man named Victor D. Chambers, who said that he had been born on the battlefield to a woman who had arrived there the night before the bloody conflict, after a long, tortuous escape from life as a slave on a southern Virginia plantation. The letter also evoked memories of war that Mr. Carroll had not talked about for over seventy years.

In an envelope whose carefully printed address closely resembled calligraphy was a letter whose flowing script bore the flourishes of handwriting styles characteristic of the late nineteenth and early twentieth centuries. The letter[1] read:

> Mr. Michael Carroll
> Dear Sir,
> I have just been looking at a picture of you in the *Evening Bulletin,* and it puts me to thinking. I remember you way back in 1910 when I was janitor of Point Street Grammar School with James M. Sawin, after Tom Brown died. Don't you remember I was put in by Frank Foss in Tom's place?
> I am really glad to know you are living and quite well.
> Now here is what I want to get at.
> I never knew before last night <u>you</u> were a Grand Army man. And may <u>God bless you</u> forever and ever! For if it had not been for <u>you</u> and thousands like you, <u>I</u> would now be in slavery.
> Listen!! My Mother when a little girl <u>in 1827</u> was stolen from Pennsylvania and sold in the slave markets of Richmond Va. She was bought by a planter down James River at City Point, who was the uncle of General Barksdale, who was killed while lead-

ing a charge upon the works of the Second Corps at Gettysburg, July 2nd 1863—Hancock's Corps.

My mother ran away from the Barksdale plantation and started for the north. She arrived at the town of Gettysburg Adams County Pa on the evening of Tuesday June 30th 1863. On Wednesday morning, July first, she started to leave the place, but was overtaken by the advance of Buford's cavalry just westward of Gettysburg on the Chambersburg Turn Pike. She could go no farther.

Mother has told me that from where she stood she could see the advancing regiments of A.P. Hill's Corps of 35,000 men, approaching from the North West. She was talking to General John F. Reynolds when he was shot from his horse, just south of the Chambersburg Road. He was telling her to get out from under the trees, for she might be killed. He fell into her arms from his horse. She broke the fall.

My mother could not get away from the field. After the 3 days fight was over, she wandered over the bloody field everywhere looking at the dead and wounded. I have heard her say many a time it was hell, hell. Once seen, <u>never</u> forgotten. Dead men, dead horses, wounded and dying men wherever she went. She was giving a poor soldier a drink, and he died with the first swallow.

I was born on the battle field of Gettysburg July 7th 1863, 4 days after the fight. I was born in an old army wagon that had all the wheels shot off it and the 6 mules were lying in the harness just as they had been killed.

No doctors, no marble slabs, no hot water, no medicines, no one but <u>God</u> and my mother. And I will be 68 years old this July 7th. Think of it!

I was born near the place where Longstreet cut through Sickles' line at the Peach Orchard. I believe every word you say when I read it here in the paper, that your Regiment of the 3rd Corps went into action 349 strong and at roll call answered only 108. <u>Noble</u> 3rd.

You have the courage, and I hope <u>God</u> will give you strength to march this Decoration Day.

I have been to Gettysburg with Mother 4 times and she has pointed out the places where men were piled 10 high at the Bloody Angle and Devil's Den.

How fearful must have been the fight when your regiment met Hood at Weed's Hill, and Sickles' line was forced back to the Wentz House. My mother has shown me where the old glorious Third stood. I have heard her say that in the yard of a Trostle near Weed's Hill she stood and counted 203 dead alone, and that was nothing!

At my mother's first lecture on the Battle of Gettysburg at the Academy of Music at Philadelphia, were seated on the stage Generals Sickles, Howard, Hancock, Slocum, Kirkpatrick, R. Penn Smith, Sheridan, (also) John Wannamaker [sic], Custer, Buffalo Bill Cody, Col. Henry R. Bliss PA 97th vol, and Ex Gov Andrew G. Curtin, state of PA (Civil War Governor).

I have said nothing, only I did not expect to say but a line or two, but when I start I most forget to quit. I was at Gettysburg on her 50th anniversary of the battle 1913. I heard that old rebel yell when they made the supposed charge across the wheat field against the Union left center. They hated you in '63. They hate you now.

Good bye
Respectfully,
Victor D. Chambers
20 Lester Street, Providence R.I.

If I was a respected Union Soldier as I know <u>you</u> are, while there was a rebel soldier wearing the gray in Dixie, I would <u>never</u> acknowledge him as my equal as a "Veteran", wearing the uniform of <u>the C.S.A.</u>

No Sir
<u>Never Never Never.</u>

My great-grandfather, who must have been intrigued by this letter, and no doubt unable to fathom all of its contents, invited Mr. Chambers to visit him. He received a second letter from Mr. Chambers, dated June 8, which read:

My Dear Mr. Carroll,
Your letter of June 3rd received and contents duly read and noted. Will say I was more than pleased to receive a return communication from you, and glad to hear that you are enjoying good health for one of your age.

I knew you [word encircled] would have the courage to be in

line on Decoration Day, for it was backed by the spirit of the days of '62. I went to Philadelphia Pa, my home city, for decoration. I went to place flowers on my Mother's and Grandmother's graves. My Grandmother was born in Port au Prince, Hayti, January 1st 1787 and died Jan 2nd 1884—age 97 years. She came to Philadelphia with her father and mother in 1793 and used to see Washington when he was President riding on horseback through the city streets.

She grew to be a woman and was married and went to live on a farm in the country. My mother was stolen from her in 1827 and sold into slavery at Richmond Va, and Grandmother saw her no more for 37 years.

My uncle, the late Joseph H. Banks of 101 Grove Street this city, and the late James C. LeCount (I guess you knew both of them) were both slaves on the Barksdale plantation at City Point, Va. Mother was well acquainted with young Massa Will Barksdale who commanded a brigade in Longstreet's Corps. And was killed at Gettysburg July 2nd. Now here is a funny but true story.

Do you know that the janitor, whose name was Armstead Lewis, and lived on Logan Avenue, South Prov, was the last janitor to have this school before me,—And he was the body servant of the Rebel General J. B. Hood, and was with him at Gettysburg. I have his old Bible here now. He had it in his pocket on that memorable Thursday afternoon. Hood's Texans were cutting you all to pieces at the Trostle House, the Peach Orchard, the Wheat Field and Little Round Top. Mr. Lewis told me that Gen. Hood swore oaths of a terrible hue, when he saw the old Sixth Corps coming down the Baltimore Pike under Sedgwick. And it saved the day. Mother says dead men were piled up in heaps like bound sheaves of wheat in the harvest field.

Wounded soldiers were lying where they had fallen 2 days previous, crying for water and slowly bleeding to death. And the temperature all 3 days stood 95 in the shade. Mr. Carroll, you were there, you know it.

So kind of you to extend to me an invitation to call on you. I feel, and as my mother has said to me oh so often, that every [word underlined twice] Colored American owes a deabt [sic] of gratitude forever [word underlined twice and encircled] to the

veteran soldiers of the Grand Army of the Republic. If nothing
happens, I will call to see you for a little chat on Tuesday afternoon July 7th, my birthday.
  Respectfully V. Chambers
  Mr. Carroll PS—Do you know Charlie Bullock?

The "little chat" between the two men eventually led to many
more visits. Mr. Carroll was at that time living with his son William,
whose daughter Harriet, my mother, was responsible for many care-
giving tasks for her frail and nearly blind ninety-one-year-old grandfather. Harriet wrote his letters and read Mr. Chamber's letters aloud
to him. She said that her grandfather rarely, if ever, talked about his
Civil War experiences with his family, who learned more from the
Evening Bulletin article than he had ever shared with them. According
to my mother, her grandfather had finally found in Victor Chambers
the one person in whom he could confide those age-encrusted
thoughts and memories. She added that the old man would hold
tightly onto the younger man's hand as they talked, in order to reinforce his concentration on every word the two exchanged.

The letters from Victor Chambers became my mother's legacy from
her grandfather, along with some of his Civil War medals and pictures. Even though I have read the letters many times before, I believe
I have only recently appreciated Mr. Chambers's passionate entreaty:
"Now here is what I want to get at. . . . Listen!!" By doing just that,
by trying to find out what Mr. Chambers wanted to convey, I discov-
ered that there is more in these letters than the story of one heroic
woman and her devoted son. Rather, they represent the history of a
whole family, and of a whole people as well.

The task of dissecting what is stated in the letters and probing into
what lies behind the words was for me very much like the painstak-
ing but exhilarating work of those scientists who devote themselves
to deciphering the secrets hidden within the earth's crust. By studying the variations and anomalies evident in strata of rock or arctic ice,
or lines within the trunks of old trees, scientists can identify periods
of drought, prolonged fire, cataclysmic movements of the earth, or
other natural phenomena that can cause severe stress. In the same
way, particular lines of Victor Chambers's letters, despite their brevi-

Note from Victor Chambers to Michael Carroll, dated June 10, 1931

ty and lack of detail, shed light not only onto the lives of the individuals described in the letters but also onto upheavals and anomalies in our nation's history that affected thousands of people.

Despite intense research and probing, with the generous assistance of knowledgeable curators, genealogists, and historians, many facts, including the first name of Victor Chambers's mother, remain unknown or unclear. I nonetheless managed to fill in many of the blanks by perusing valuable firsthand accounts, especially many volumes of slave testimony and official records of names and events covered in the letters. This same research also yielded fascinating information about the author of the letters, whose life bears witness to the love he had for his mother and for those who fought to ensure his freedom.

Because the only primary material on which I could draw was the letters themselves, I was often limited to informed conjecture, surmising or imagining certain thoughts or actions, by placing Mr. Chambers's elliptical phrases in the context of what was said, thought, or done by others whose testimony has been recorded.

While this can never be completely satisfactory, I concluded that this would be preferable to fictionalizing any part of this story. To opt for the latter course would be a betrayal of the inherent honor and decency that characterize Mr. Chambers's letters. I therefore entreat readers to bear with my use of phrases such as "Victor's mother may have" or "might have" experienced various thoughts or deeds. Extrapolating from factual statements made by other former slaves, and imagining them to be similar to those of Victor's mother, is the closest one can come to gaining some insight into those portions of her life which remain unknown.

Trying to peer into the dim distances to the African heritage of people such as Victor Chambers is obviously an impossible task. I did, however, desire to show the links between belief systems and artistic expression of American slaves and their African forebears. After researching the vast richness of the various African civilizations, I decided, for the sake of consistency, to use the culture of Dahomey to show these links. Dahomey, now known as Benin, was the point where those soon-to-be slaves (including Victor Chambers's grand-mother and her parents) were boarded on French ships bound for Haiti. While many of these people were actually from Dahomey, many more were sent there from throughout Africa for onward ship-ment to the Americas.

There is in the ancestral cults and literature of Dahomey so much that seems to intersect and coincide with the fate of Victor Chambers's forebears and others lost during the African diaspora. The themes of Dahomean poetry have great resonance with the sorrow songs created by American slaves. For example, the following poem uncannily hints at the fate of generations that would be lost forever:

> An old woman weeps
> Amidst the leaves; she weeps
> Amidst the leaves of the forest.
> And she says, "The birds in the bush,
>
> The lives of these birds are to be envied.
> How is it that man born into life
> Has no more generations?
> He has no more."
> (Herskovitz, *Dahomey*, 1:380)

I believe that the references I include to Dahomean history and culture bring a richness to this story. The beauty of the rituals associated with that culture especially inspired me to create the one fictionalized chapter, the epilogue.

Despite the absence of details such as their origins, the story of Victor Chambers and his mother, as recounted in his letters, has its own integrity and truth. A clearly delineated, factually complete account of this or any family would perhaps be interesting to genealogists but would probably make for dull reading. I believe that the presence of the unknown, the secret, and thus the sacred in this story will attract and perhaps inspire readers. It is a story that deserves to be told, for it has much to teach this and future generations about the nobility of spirit and desire for freedom that characterized thousands of heroic men and women and enabled them to transcend terrible dehumanization and suffering.

Finally, a note about language: In quoting the words of former slaves, I chose to use spelling, syntax, and punctuation that would be understood by readers today. Abolitionists and others who recorded the interviews of former slaves, and the speeches of well-known individuals such as Harriet Tubman and Sojourner Truth, often used distorted forms of what they considered to be slave dialect (words such as "dis," "de," "chilluns," etc.). There are at least three versions of the famous phrase attributed to Sojourner Truth: "Aren't I a woman?", "Ar'nt I a woman?", or "Ain't I a woman?" Whether or not she actually spoke those words, and however the words are transcribed,[2] her message was, and still is, clearly understood.

John Blassingame, editor and compiler of slave narratives, interviews and speeches, noted that he often found several versions of the same narrative, varying according to the way the transcriber believed slaves pronounced words. He noted that, even in the case of slaves who spoke English perfectly, their interviews were changed into a crude form of Southern speech associated with slaves.[3] It has always been a difficult decision, in using transcriptions of slaves' words, as to whether one should perpetuate those distortions or "sanitize" them in some way. Author Leon Litwack, for example, said that he made "no attempt to alter the transcription of Negro dialect, even in those instances where the white man's perception of black language seems obviously and intentionally distorted,"[4] to avoid creating yet another distortion.

My intention here is neither to "sanitize" nor distort, but rather to ensure that readers comprehend the full impact of what those former slaves, whose words have been preserved and recorded, have to say about the experience of slavery. Just as in the case of Sojourner Truth, their voices and, more importantly, their message, still resonate today.

xviii

Victor Chambers's first letter to Michael Carroll, dated May 14, 1931

2

I am really glad to know
you are liveing and
quite well,
Now here is what I want
to get at,
I never knew before last
night you were a
Grand Army Man.
And May God bless you
forever and ever,
For if it had not been
for you and thousands
like you, I would now
be in slavery

3

Listen, "My mother when a little girl in 1827 was stolen from Pennsylvania and sold in the slave markets of Richmond Va. She was bought by a planter down James River at City Point ☆ who was the Uncle of General Barksdale who was killed while leading a charge upon the works of the Second Corps at Gettysburg July 2nd/1863 Hancocks Corps

4

My mother ran away from Barksdales plantation and started for the north. She arrived at the town of Gettysburg Adams County Pa on the evening of Tuesday June 30th 1863 On Wednesday morning July first she started to leave the place, but was overtaken by the advance of Bufords cavalry just westward of Gettysburg on the Chambersburg Turn Pike. she could go no farther.

Mother has told me that
from where she stood she
could see the advancing
Regiments of A, P. Hills Corps
of 35 000 men, approaching
from the North West.

She was talking to General
John F. Reynolds when he
was shot from his horse
just south of the
Chambersburg Road.

"He was telling her to get
out from under the trees
for she might be killed.
He fell into her arms from
his horse, she broke the fall.

6

My mother could not
git away from the field.
After the 3 days fight,
was over, she wandered
over the bloody field
every where, looking at
the dead and wounded
I have heard her say many
a time it was hell, hell,
once seen, never forgotten,
Dead men, dead horses
wounded and dying men
where ever she went
she was giving a poor
soldier a drink, and he
died with the first swallow.

7

I was born on the
battle field of
Gettysburg July 7th 1863
4 days after the fight
I was born in an old
army wagon that had all
the wheels shot off it
and the 6 mules were
lying in the harness just
as they had been killed
No Doctors, no marble Slabs,
no Hot Water, no medicines.
No one but God and my
mother. And I will be
68 years old this July 7th
think of it.

8

I was born near the
place where Longstreet
cut through Sickles
line at the Peach Orchard,
I believe every word you
say when I read it here
in the paper that your
Regiment of the 3 rd corps
went into action 3 49 strong
and at roll call answered
only 1 0 8, Noble 3 0 0

you have the courage, and
I hope God will give you
strength to march this
Decoration day.

I have been to Gettysburg
with mother 4 times and
she has pointed out the places
where men were piled 10 high
at the Bloody Angle and
Devils Den

How fearful must have
been the fight when your
regiment met Hood at
Weeds Hill, and Sickles
line was forced back to
the Wentz House, My mother
has shown me, where the
old glorious Third stood

I have heard her say
that in the yard of
a Trostle near Weeds Hill

she stood and counted
203 dead alone, and
that was nothing.
At my mother's first lecture
on the Battle of Gettysburg,
at the Academy of Music
at Philadelphia, were seated
on the stage Generals

Sickles   Howard
Hancock   Slocum

Kirkpatrick   R Penn Smith
Sheridan   John Wannamaker
Custer   Buffalo Bill Cody
Col Henry Q Gross Pa 97 vol
and Ex Gov Andrew G Curtin
state of Pa   (Civil war
Governor)

11

I have said nothing
only, L ≡Did not expect to
say but a line or too.
but when I start I most
forget to quit, I was at
Gettysburg on her 50TH
anniversary of the battle 1913
I heard that old rebel yell
when they made the supposed
charge across the wheat field
against the Union left center
They hated you in 63 They
hate you now.
Good bye
Cap Fuller

Victor D Chambers
20 Lester St Providence
    D D

12

If I was a respected
Union Soldier, as I
know <u>you</u> are,
While there was a rebel
soldier wearing the gray
in Dixie
I would <u>never</u> acknowledge
him as my equal as a
Veteran, wearing the
uniform of the C.S.A,
No Sir
Never never never.

1.

Providence, June 8th

My Dear Mr Carroll

Your letter of June 3rd
received and contents duly
read and noted.

Will say I was more than
pleased to receive a retourn
communication from you,

And glad to hear you are
enjoying good health for one
of your age,

I knew (you) would have
the courage to bein line
on Decoration day,
for it was backed by the
spirit of the days of 62

I went to Philadelphia Pa
my home City for decoration,

Victor Chambers's second letter to Michael Carroll, dated June 8 [1931]

2.

I went to place flowers on my
Mothers and Grandmothers graves.
My Grandmother was born in Port Au Prince
Hayti   January 1st 1787 and died
Jan 2nd 1884 age 97 years.
She came to Philadelphia with
her father and mother in 1793
And used to see Washington
when he was President riding
on horseback Through the
city streets.
She grew to be a woman and
was married and went to
live on a farm in the country,
My mother was stolen from
her in 1827 and sold into
slavery at Richmond Va
and Grandmother saw her
no more for 87 years.

<u>3</u>

My Uncle the late Joseph H.
Banks of 101 Grove street
This city and the late James
C. LeCount (I guess you knew
both of them) were both slaves on the
Barksdale plantation at
City Point = Va. Mother was
well acquainted with young
massa Will Barksdale who
commanded a brigade in
Longstreets Corps. And was
killed at Gettysburg July 2nd
Now here is a funny but true
story.

Do you know That the
Janitor, whose name was
Armstead Lewis, and lived
on Logan Avenue South Grove,
was the last janitor to have
This School before me; —

4.

And he was the body servant of the
Rebel General J B Hood and
was with him at Gettysburg
I have his old Bible here now.
He had it in his pocket on that
memorable Thursday afternoon.
Hoods Texans were cutting you
all topieces at the Trostle House
The Peach Orchard The wheat
field and Little Round Top,
Mr Lewis told me that Gen
Hood swore oathes of a
terrible hue, when he saw
The old sixth Corps comeing
down The Baltimore Pike
under Sedgwick. And it
saved The day. Mother says
dead men were piled up in
heaps like bound sheaves of
wheat in The harvest field

5

wounded soldiers were lying
where they had fallen 2 days
previous crying for water
and slowly bleeding to death
And The temperature all 3
days stood 95° in The shade
Mr Carroll you were there, you
Know it,

So kind of you to extend to me an
invitation to call on you I feel, and
as my mother has said to me oh so
often, That every Colored American
owes a deabt of gratitude forever
to The veteran soldiers of The
Grand Army of The Republic
If nothing happens I will call to see you
for a little chat on Tuesday afternoon
July 7th my birthday.
                    respectfully W Chambers
  Mr Carroll
P.S. Do you know Charlie Bullock?

A
C
K
N
O
W
L
E
D
G
M
E
N
T
S

Many institutions and individuals provided invaluable assistance in carrying out the research needed for undertaking this project. While it is not possible to list them all, I wish to thank the following individuals for the information and other substantive assistance they provided: Charles L. Blockson of the Blockson Afro-American Collection at Temple University and author of definitive works on the Underground Railroad as well as on African-American genealogy; the Honorable Ruth Davis, Distinguished Advisor for International Affairs at Howard University and former United States Ambassador to Benin; Professor Allen B. Ballard, Department of Africana Studies at the University at Albany, State University of New York; Mark Dunkelman, Civil War historian and president of the Rhode Island Civil War Round Table; Gary B. Nash, professor of history at the University of California, Los Angeles, and director of the National Center for History in the Schools; Andrew J. Boisvert of the Rhode Island Historical Society; Joachina Bela Teixeira, executive director of the Rhode Island Black Heritage Society; Laura Beardsley of the Historical Society of Pennsylvania; Philip Lapsansky of the Library

Company of Philadelphia; Renee Carey of the Chester County Historical Society, West Chester, Pennsylvania; Kathy Georg-Harrison, senior historian, Gettysburg National Park; Louise Arnold French of the United States Army Military History Institute in Carlisle, Pennsylvania; Brigadier General (Ret.) Hal Larson, U.S. army historian, Carlisle, Pennsylvania; Timothy Smith, licensed Gettysburg battlefield guide; Peter Vermilyea of the Civil War Institute at Gettysburg College; Al Smith of the Library of Congress; Suzanne S. Levy, Virginia Room Librarian, Fairfax County Public Library, Fairfax, Virginia; Jean Odom of St. Paul's A.M.E. Church in Gettysburg; Julia Carrington, genealogist in South Boston, Virginia; LaReine S. Sabella, M.D., obstetrician and my source of information about nineteenth-century birthing practices; the late Andrew J. Bell of Providence, Rhode Island; and Cynthia Ross Meeks, artist and descendent of the family whose members included Victor Chambers's second wife, Selena, and the sculptor Nancy Elizabeth Prophet.

Because the world of publishing was new to me, I greatly appreciated the support and enthusiasm of Markus Wiener for this project. I am also indebted to Willa Speiser, who edited my work with tact, skill, and patience. It was a pleasure to work with her and others associated with Markus Wiener Publishers.

I must also acknowledge friends who supported and challenged me with their insightful recommendations with regard to style and content, especially V. James Fazio, Bettie Clark, Agnes Gavin, and Antionetta Lee. Everett Lewis and Pat Chaney provided much-needed format support. I owe much gratitude to my sister, Carrolle M. Rinaldi, whose collaboration and encouragement sustained me during the many years of research and revision involved in the preparation of this book.

Michael Carroll in 1862

CHRONOLOGY OF EVENTS

1780   Pennsylvania passes Gradual Abolition Act

1793   United States Congress passes Fugitive Slave Act
        Slave revolts in Haiti
        Victor Chambers's great-grandparents leave Haiti for
            Philadelphia

1821   Birth of Confederate General William Barksdale

1827   Victor Chambers's mother kidnapped, sold in Richmond
            slave markets and bought by William Barksdale's uncle

1863   Victor's mother escapes, arrives at Gettysburg June 30
            Battle begins July 1, ends July 3
        Victor Chambers born on Gettysburg battlefield July 7

1865   Civil War ends

1876   United States Centennial Exposition in Philadelphia

1898   Victor Chambers moves to Rhode Island

1913   Fiftieth anniversary of Gettysburg

1931   Victor Chambers reads about Civil War veteran Michael
            Carroll and writes to him

1933   Michael Carroll dies

1943   Victor Chambers dies

"The dream and the hope of the slave"

1

Bringing the gifts that
my ancestors gave
I am the dream and the
hope of the slave. I rise.
—*Maya Angelou, "Still I Rise"*

Despite their brevity, Mr. Chambers's references to his grandmother and great-grandparents nonetheless provide sufficient clues as to where his forebears came from and under what circumstances they arrived in Philadelphia.

> My grandmother was born in Port au Prince, Hayti, January 1st, 1787, and died January 2nd, 1884—age 97 years. She came to Philadelphia with her father and mother in 1793, and used to see Washington when he was President, riding on horseback through the city streets.

The mention of the specific year 1793 was a valuable clue regarding Victor Chambers's great-grandparents. In 1793 there was a great exodus to the United States of French refugees from Saint Domingue (as Haiti was called prior to independence in 1804) in the wake of violent slave rebellions on that island. Fleeing for their lives, the French sought refuge at various ports along the east coast. Among the refugees who landed in Philadelphia in the summer of 1793 were about five hundred domestic slaves brought to the United States by their owners, as well as a small number of free blacks, and about seventy free *gens de couleur* (light-skinned people of mixed race; literally, "people of color"). In all, more than three thousand French-speaking refugees from Saint Domingue would arrive in Philadelphia by the end of 1794. Of this total, approximately eight hundred refugees of African ancestry would augment the city's total black population by about 25 percent.[1]

I was not able to ascertain whether Victor's great-grandparents came to Philadelphia as slaves, free blacks, or free *gens de couleur*. Many historical accounts fail to differentiate among these groups, instead lumping all the nonwhite refugees into one class of impoverished, sickly, and uneducated people; often, they are merely included under generic headings. Historian Gary Nash, who did perhaps the most definitive studies of the refugees from Saint Domingue, said that "no accurate census of French West Indies refugees exists . . . [and that] the commonly cited estimate of 10,000 is most likely considerably short of the total number."[2] Registers of the Port of Philadelphia list the names of white passengers arriving from the West Indies, as well as the names of some free blacks, and specify only the numbers, but not names, of slaves brought by each owner. Passenger lists for the year 1793 indicate that such 158 ships arrived in Philadelphia, bearing 1,659 white passengers, 29 "freed negroes," and 629 slaves.

After six months, slaves who arrived in Philadelphia were issued manumission documents. Because many of the slaves were young, unaccompanied, and spoke no English, they immediately signed on as indentured servants to their former owners. I found that perusing the manumission documents compiled by the Philadelphia Abolitionist Society was as futile as studying the port documents in my search for Victor Chambers's great-grandparents and their six-year-old daughter. Because most people are merely listed by first name, or grouped together by number only as the slaves of particular owners, it was impossible to discern a family grouping of a mother, father, and six-year-old daughter. I even contacted Gary Nash in my quest for this family. After a thorough review of his index cards and notes, he told me that he could not identify any easily discernible family of three. He also noted that there are many gaps in the port

Slaves being loaded onto ships

documents. We will never know, then, whether Victor Chambers's forebears arrived as free blacks or as slaves, who either opted for freedom in Philadelphia or chose to work as indentured servants.

Prior to coming to Philadelphia with their owners, African slaves in Haiti had come mainly from Dahomey (now Benin) on French slave ships. Dahomey had long been a lively center for artists, artisans, and craftsmen; it was a place where women served not only as priestesses in cults such as *vodou* (from the Fon word *vodun,* or "deity") but also as soldiers famed for their bravery, referred to in European sailors' legendary accounts as the "Amazons" of Dahomey. Like other areas of West Africa, Dahomey had many cults based on the belief that a person would ultimately join the company of his ancestors after death and would, in turn, be deified and worshiped by his own descendants. The associated belief that each person carries within him the souls of those who preceded him, and that each person is a living part of the larger ancestral soul, fortified those ultimately sold into bondage. This belief system enabled them not only to endure, but also to rise above, the suffering and indignity forced upon them.[3]

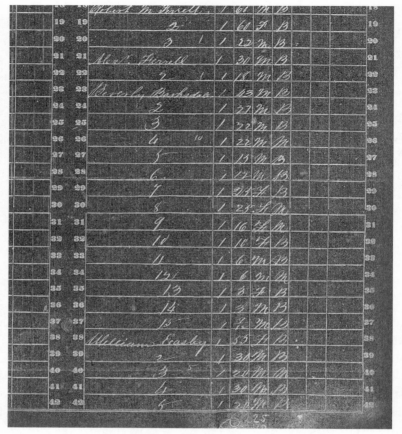

Inventory listing slaves of Beverly Barksdale

While reading about the Dahomean belief systems, I noted one practice that seemed particularly significant in the context of my search for the first name of Victor Chambers's mother. While I did ascertain that her last name was indeed Chambers, I never found any record of her first name. For example, the slave schedules for the area where she was ultimately enslaved do not include names; all that is listed are the owner's name and the sex (M or F), color (B or M, for black or mulatto), and approximate age of each slave. In Dahomey, when a child was born, the mother gave her baby a name that she would hold in complete secrecy and never mention aloud as long as the child lived. While other names would come later, this secret name had to be guarded at all costs by the mother as a special magic or protection against evil, and against those who might steal the soul of a person and enslave it for evil purposes.[4] Also, in the culture of Dahomey in particular, a woman's name was held to be sacred and rarely mentioned. A husband usually referred to his wife in public by the Fon language word *asichi* (a generic term for "wife"). During the marriage ceremony, a man invented a new name for his wife; henceforth, she would be addressed by that name in private, both by her husband and her friends. Her original name would never again be spoken. At public ceremonies, women—especially pregnant women —would be addressed by the rueful *ma yolo ni che* ("Do not call my name").[5]

While I was continually frustrated in my efforts to find Victor Chambers's mother's first name, perhaps this is what she would have preferred, given the West African practice of using the secret name to protect one's soul and the Dahomean practice of concealing a woman's name. Also, I believe that her most treasured means of identity would always be that of Victor Chambers's mother, rather than the plaintive "Do not call my name," a term that seems so apt for women whose identities were lost during the upheavals of slavery. In reading the testimony of those who survived slavery in the American South, I found that many men refrained from mentioning their mothers by name, as if to protect them from the horrors they had endured. It does not seem strange to me, therefore, that Victor Chambers never mentioned his mother's first name in the letters, since that might have been too intimate, and even sacred, to share with a stranger such as my great-grandfather.

People taken to Saint Domingue as slaves spent terrifying nights and days chained and living in squalid, inhuman conditions on French slave ships. Those who survived the crossing found themselves strangers in an inhospitable land where conditions were not much better than on board the crowded ships. Their lives on the huge French tobacco and sugarcane plantations were usually of short

Inside a slave ship

duration, but that did not matter to the French owners, who constantly brought in new slaves by the thousands. About ten to fifteen thousand slaves were brought in each year; in 1787, more than forty thousand were brought to the island.[6]

When I visited Haiti, particularly the area where Victor's great-grandparents lived, I was struck by the name given to the barren and arid depression in the center of the island, where Port au Prince is located; namely, the Cul de Sac, which means "Dead End" and which truly represented just that for so many slaves. Then as now, little rain fell in this valley located between foreboding black mountain ranges. The area and its inhabitants suffered under prolonged droughts, devastating hurricanes, and the constant threat of earthquakes. Slaves working in this valley of death frequently succumbed to malaria, yellow fever, malnutrition, and abuse. As they died, more came to replace them. Large numbers of slaves were needed to maintain the levels of sugar and coffee production that world markets and the French court demanded. The sugar trade was especially important to the French, since about half of the world's sugar came from plantations in Saint Domingue.

This Caribbean island was an idyllic paradise for the wealthy French plantation owners, whose palatial homes and surroundings contrasted starkly with the squalor of the slaves' huts. Ships bearing tobacco and sugar to France regularly returned laden with luxury goods of all kinds to be placed in the planters' mansions, which were usually set on mountain terraces and surrounded by landscaped gardens. Many of these still exist and attest to the glory of that era. To reach them, one usually follows a broad avenue framed by orange-colored flame trees, or *flamboyantes*. Although many of the mansions are overgrown today, one can see the outlines of the formal gardens that once were filled with exotic flowers indigenous to the island.

Despite this opulence, French women for the most part found the climate oppressive and spent most of the year in France, where the children were educated. The husbands consoled themselves at the island's numerous dance halls, gambling dens, and brothels. In taking on black or mixed-race mistresses, the French planters gave rise to the development of a whole new social class—namely, the *gens de couleur*. Their political views usually reflected the royalist tendencies of the white planters, and they looked with disdain on the free blacks and slaves. Well-to-do *gens de couleur* sent their children to France to be educated. They were proud of their heritage and had political clout they could call upon if needed. Among their influential supporters in the French legislature was the Marquis de Lafayette. In 1791, largely as a result of his intervention, the Constituent Assembly in Paris granted Haiti's *gens de couleur* French citizenship. By that time, the island contained about 28,000 whites, 22,000 *gens de couleur*, and about 400,000 black people—most of whom were slaves.[7]

Among the slave population, those considered more intelligent and presentable were trained as house servants, while those sent to work in the sugarcane and tobacco fields lived in filthy, primitive huts with only meager food allotments for subsistence. In the tobacco fields, women and men performed the same backbreaking tasks. On the sugar plantations, men were usually assigned to labor away from the cane fields as blacksmiths, carpenters, sugar boilers, or irrigation workers, while the women bore the brunt of labor in the searing sun of the fields, where their skin would be cut by the sharp canes and where blood-thirsty ants and disease-bearing mosquitoes pestered them constantly.

One history of life in Saint Domingue described "the cracks of the whip, the stifled cries, and the heavy groans of the Negroes [that] characterized daybreak" on the plantations.[8] Like their counterparts on plantations in the American South, the French owners used many tactics to subdue recalcitrant slaves, including religion. Catholicism was the only religion allowed in the island; *vodou* and other African religious practices had to be kept secret. If slaves were not obedient, priests would excommunicate them and try to convince them that they were destined for eternal damnation. Like many clergymen in the American South, Catholic priests in Saint Domingue regularly gave sermons stressing the unworthiness of the slave and the superiority of the master.[9]

Even though there were weak regulations allegedly promulgated to protect slaves, it was legal for the French owners to torture and sentence to death any slaves engaging in rebellious practices. Their methods of torture and death were perhaps even more horrendous than those practiced by American slave owners, and included burning slaves alive; filling them with gunpowder and blowing them up; burning the feet, legs, and arms while the slaves were gagged and unable to cry out; whipping the slaves almost to the point of death; making the slaves eat their own excrement; and mutilating or cutting off ears or limbs.[10]

By the late 1700s, after nearly two centuries of slavery on the island, the slaves were preparing for a day of reckoning. The tide of revolution, which was rising violently in France, would soon wash over the island with the force of a devastating hurricane. People of all colors and social classes knew what was happening abroad. Domestic slaves overheard conversations in their masters' salons and dining rooms and spread the word to slaves in the fields. The free blacks and *gens de couleur* who frequented the cafés of Port au Prince and Cap Français openly discussed the egalitarian ideas of Rousseau and other French philosophers. Among those inspired by such ideas was François-Dominique Toussaint, who had been born a slave but gained his freedom and eventually led the slave revolt of 1791, under the name of Toussaint Louverture. People in the salons and cafés also discussed the revolution in North America and were proud of the role played by the Marquis de Lafayette, who would later, in collaboration with Jefferson, draft that great French charter of democracy, liberty, and equality known as the Declaration of the Rights of Man.

Black residents of Saint Domingue rejoiced as they learned of the bloody scenes at the guillotine in Paris in 1789. The white plantation owners and most *gens de couleur,* however, observed the events with apprehension. It would not be long before rebellious Jacobins from Paris arrived in Saint Domingue to assist the uprising of black slaves

Artist's depiction of a battle between French soldiers and Haitian rebels during the Haitian revolution

on the island. Many were dismembered or cut in half, with the mutilated remains displayed on public fences and posts.[11] Among the rebellious slaves were many women, who fought as fiercely as the "Amazons" of Dahomey.

The rising tide of revolt reached massive proportions in June 1793, culminating in a devastating, bloody attack at Cap Français, in which more than five thousand French men, women, and children were killed.[12] After this, the terrified French planters and *gens de couleur* knew they had no recourse but to leave the island for ports in the United States. Even in the midst of their confusion and terror, French planters headed for Philadelphia found the time to send petitions to the Pennsylvania Assembly concerning their domestic slaves, seeking their exemption from that state's Gradual Abolition Act of 1780, which specified that any slave brought into that state would automatically be freed after six months.[13] Thanks to heavy lobbying by free blacks and abolitionists in Pennsylvania, however, the plantation owners' petition was denied. Nevertheless, the exact legal status of slaves from Saint Domingue would not be clarified for many years, and they lived in a state of limbo where they were neither completely enslaved nor completely free.[14]

Slaves sailing aboard the ships bound for North America were filled with hope and the anticipation that they would soon be free. Somewhere in that flotilla of merchant ships and boats heading northward, under the guiding light of the North Star, was Victor Chambers's grandmother, then just a little girl of six, with her parents. She never would have imagined then that more than thirty years later, her own child would be carried along on these same waters. But that child—flesh of her flesh, bone of her bone, and bearer of the dreams and spirits of her ancestors—would be sailing south rather than north and many years later would ultimately return northward, under the guidance of the North Star.

"Thou art a little slave, my child"

2

Oh, child! Thou art a little slave.
Thou art a little slave, my child,
And much I grieve and mourne
That so dark a destiny [befell]
The lovely babe I'd borne.
—*"Mother's Lament," slave song*

When the six-year-old girl and her parents arrived in Philadelphia, they would soon discover that this capital of the United States was neither the utopian paradise nor the city of brotherly love they may have dreamed of. Rather, what they found was a pestilence-ridden, polluted inferno where fires burned night and day, guns and cannons were fired into the air at all hours, and people were dying in the streets.

By the summer of 1793, America's capital was probably the nation's dampest, least healthy, and most polluted city, and many of the refugees died of respiratory problems shortly after their arrival. Beneath the city were swamps, marshes, pools of clay pits and stagnant water, and there was only one sewer. Noxious fumes wafted continuously from holes dug in the streets to collect water from the gutters.[1] The part of the city in which most of the refugees from Saint Domingue settled was close to the Delaware River, in what is now a designated historic district. Many of these streets are still paved with cobblestones, and the original buildings, now restored to modern standards of gentility, still stand. Nevertheless, one can still find some of the holes and trenches from which poisonous fumes and waste once flowed.

11

Lithograph of Philadelphia's Delaware River waterfront at Walnut Street, ca. 1835

Before Victor's grandmother and her parents could really begin their new lives, they were caught up in a catastrophe that almost devastated the city of Philadelphia. Although they and other people from the West Indies were familiar with yellow fever, they were not prepared for its overwhelming effect on this North American city, nor for the dangerous and frightening measures taken to combat it. Because the outbreak occurred shortly after the influx of such a large number of refugees from Saint Domingue, Philadelphians were only too ready to blame the epidemic on them; many of the newcomers were indeed gaunt and sickly and spoke of similar outbreaks on the island. To the amusement of the French refugees, some of the city's Quakers blamed the epidemic on a decline in morals within the city.[2]

This outbreak should not have come as a complete surprise to Philadelphians and, in fact, should have been expected. Every decade for about seventy years, yellow fever had struck the city, with each outbreak more dreadful than the last. By 1793, the city had been free of the pestilence for about fifteen years, so its next visitation was overdue, and, in fact, there were signs of its impending arrival. The preceding winter had been unseasonably warm, and the spring weather was uncommonly hot and wet, with streams and rivers overflowing and creating swamplike conditions in the city's streets and alleys. The summer was hotter and drier than past summers had been. Decaying remains of dead fish and animals piled up on the banks of the Delaware River and in the market area, along with the refuse of the city. People were tormented by an amazing number of flies, mosquitoes and other insects, creating what city authorities pro-claimed to be an "unwholesome atmosphere." Despite all these signs, no one was prepared for the terrible outbreak, and it was easy to blame it on the refugees.[3]

During the summer months, the disease reached epidemic propor-tions, and by September, it had overwhelmed the city's resources. This once vibrant city, then the nation's capital, looked like a ghost town, with people dead or dying in the streets and in their homes, while others, including President Washington, left for cleaner air in the country. By fall, half the city's population had either died or fled. Before the epidemic subsided with the onset of cold winter weather, the disease had claimed more than five thousand lives.[4]

During the siege, the city had taken on a frightening aspect. People seized upon any remedy rumored to alleviate their suffering. When someone claimed that smoke was a deterrent, people all over the city began puffing cigars and burning gunpowder and sulfur in their homes. At night, the whole city seemed to be on fire as streets were set ablaze with fires that authorities thought might purify the air. The mayor also ordered soldiers to fire muskets and cannons to cover the city in what he hoped would be a purifying cloud of smoke. The city's lamplighters refused to go into the waterfront area where most of the black refugees had settled, for fear of contracting the disease.[5] Conse-quently, the only illumination in this neighborhood came from the fires burning around the city.

Among the alleged cures that became popular throughout the city was garlic. People began tying it onto underwear, stuffing it in pock-ets, belts and shoes, and chewing great wads of it. Some also drank concoctions of garlic and tar water mixed with myrrh, pepper, and as much camphor as they could stand.[6] One can only imagine the fright this caused for children such as Victor's grandmother, trapped in close quarters with other refugees in a city that distrusted them and surrounded by terrifying sights, sounds, and smells.

The epidemic was seen by Philadelphia's black leaders as an oppor-tunity to demonstrate their brotherly love and compassion. Richard Allen and Absolom Jones, former slaves who became church leaders and forceful advocates for Philadelphia's black community, enlisted

Portrait of Absolom Jones,
the founding minister of Philadelphia's
first black church, the African Episcopal
Church of St. Thomas, by Raphaelle Peale

their parishioners and followers to take on the odious tasks of tending to the sick and dying by serving as nurses, death cart drivers, and gravediggers. The belief that black people were somehow immune to the disease was soon dispelled, as many of these volunteers succumbed to the illness. While most of the city's white residents were grateful to the black community for assuming tasks they were reluctant to perform, publisher Matthew Carey unleashed vicious attacks against the black volunteer workers for allegedly charging exorbitant fees for nursing the sick and tending to the dying. Most people, however, saw this as a continuation of Carey's long series of attacks against blacks in favor of Irish workers competing with blacks. Richard Allen and Absolom Jones quickly came to the defense of their followers, acknowledging that, while some black as well as white people were charging high fees for this work, their parishioners had sought no recompense for their work of compassion and heroism.[7]

Once the cold weather arrived and the epidemic subsided, city authorities and influential citizens such as Benjamin Franklin expressed their thanks to their black neighbors by contributing to the completion of a new church whose construction had been halted by the yellow fever outbreak. This church, later associated with a new denomination known as the African Methodist Episcopal (A.M.E.) Church, was, and still is, lovingly called Mother Bethel by its

*Moving the building (left) to house Bethel African Methodist Episcopal Church,
founded by Richard Allen in Philadelphia in 1794*

members. It later served as a refuge and an important stop on the Underground Railroad.

The type of reception the refugees from Saint Domingue received, and the extent to which they succeeded or failed in adjusting to life in Philadelphia, depended largely on the color of their skin. While Victor's grandmother would have been too young to notice, her parents were probably able to distinguish these differences, despite their lack of familiarity with the language spoken in the United States. The white refugees were welcomed with open arms by the large French population living in Philadelphia, and by the local press that portrayed them as victims of black violence on the island. They found an especially strong friend and advocate in Thomas Jefferson, who no doubt identified closely with them as a slave owner himself. Jefferson was deeply concerned that all the islands of the Caribbean might fall into the hands of rebellious black slaves and perhaps inspire similar actions closer to home. He petitioned successfully on behalf of the white refugees to his fellow Virginian, President James Monroe.

While the black refugees did not have such strong advocates working on their behalf, they nonetheless could look for support from two organizations that had proved of vital importance to African-Americans living in Philadelphia. The Pennsylvania Abolitionist Society (PAS), which included many Quakers and influential Philadelphians such as Benjamin Franklin, and the Free African Society (FAS), which included black leaders such as Richard Allen and Absolom Jones, had already established schools for educating black children and committees to help black workers find jobs. It was thanks to heavy lobbying by the PAS and FAS that the French slave owners were unsuccessful in their attempts to have their domestic slaves declared exempt from the Gradual Abolition Act. Although a large number of these slaves had signed on to indentured service with their former owners almost as soon as they were manumitted, they were all eventually freed because Pennsylvania's manumission laws stipulated that no slave younger than twenty-one would remain indentured for more than seven years, and any child born to indentured parents would remain a bound servant for no more than twenty-eight years.[8]

For the small percentage of free blacks who had come from Saint Domingue, as well as slaves who chose freedom over indentured service with their former owners, adjustment to their new life was extremely difficult. With the influx of the black refugees, African-Americans now counted for about 10 percent of Philadelphia's population, making this the largest black population in the country. Most of these people lived in cheap tenements that had been hastily built to deal with the city's growing population; others lived in wood shanties on the bare ground, or in damp, cold cellars. Not surprisingly, given the inadequate housing and poor ventilation, the high death rate was usually attributed to consumption and diseases of the chest.[9]

The lighter-skinned people known as *gens de couleur,* who brought with them skills, money, and political clout, fared better. For example, shortly after their arrival in Philadelphia, they sent a delegation to France to lobby successfully for the same level of monetary recompense for their losses in Saint Domingue that the white refugees received. They also blended in easily with Philadelphia's well-to-do African-American community, which included a large proportion of light-skinned people of mixed race. One group of free *gens de couleur,* together with others who had come from Haiti as slaves, found a way to thrive and find financial success. Bearing names such as Dutrieuille, Baptiste, Appo, Duterte, Montier, Cuyjet, Le Count, and Augustin, these families quickly established a virtual monopoly on the catering business in Philadelphia. They supported each other and usually married within their close-knit group. The Baptiste and Dutrieuille catering establishments, in particular, were frequented by all levels of Philadelphia society, as well as by visiting foreign dignitaries such as Lafayette.[10] Important white French and American residents vied to have the black catering establishments prepare their dinners, receptions, festive summer outdoor dances, and winter skating parties. These caterers and restaurateurs represented a set of self-reliant, creative entrepreneurs who later joined the abolitionist cause and became active in the Underground Railroad.

One sentence in Victor Chambers's obituary suggests the possibility that his great-grandparents were members of this influential group. The obituary indicated that he owned many prized possessions that had been given to his great-grandparents "by Lafayette and other dignitaries" of that era.[11] It is also possible that Victor Chambers's middle initial of "D" may have represented the name of his great-grandparents—for example, a French name beginning with a "D," as in Duterte or Dutrieuille.

While I combed through records of the important catering families at the Balch Institute and Pennsylvania Historical Society in Philadelphia, and interviewed descendants of some of the old catering families, I could not find anything that could help me link Victor to these families, but three descendants of the Dutrieuille family provided some tantalizing information that could identify a link between that prestigious family and Victor Chambers's mother. Each stated, in separate interviews, that at about the same time that Victor's mother was kidnapped, some traumatic event occurred to a branch of the family living somewhere in the Delaware/New Jersey area. No one knew what that event was, although one family member said that a kidnapping would certainly be considered traumatic for any family, but particularly for this family, which boasted of never having been affected by the scourge of slavery. The original

*Black female street vendors in Philadelphia in the early 19th century
selling "pepper pot" soup*

Dutrieuille ancestors came to Haiti from France as free people—half French and half African, specifically Dahomean.

Even if Victor Chambers's grandmother belonged to this more privileged element of society, she would not have been immune to the growing racial unrest in the city, especially the animosity of whites toward the black population. By the early 1800s, the city of Philadelphia was booming, and it became easier for black people with skills and ambition to find jobs and improve their standard of living. Black people had pride in their African heritage and often went to squares downtown to dance and sing in African languages, accompanying themselves on homemade guitars and instruments made out of gourds. In the open-air South Street market, African women, wearing flowing gowns and multicolored turbans, sold jelly doughnuts and crullers, or stirred large cauldrons of pepperpot soup.[12] White residents were becoming alarmed at the increasingly public presence of black people in their midst, and their concern grew as young black men became more boisterous, sometimes marching through the streets with swords—raising the specter of events in Saint Domingue. Black leaders tried unsuccessfully to exhort the young people to act in a more orderly manner.

In a move designed to prevent anticipated racial problems, city leaders forbade blacks to attend Philadelphia's Fourth of July celebrations. The black community soon found its own cause to celebrate when, on January 1, 1804, Saint Domingue declared its independence from France and reinstated the island's original Indian name of Haiti.[13] On that day, marked with great jubilation by the black people in Philadelphia, Victor's grandmother would have celebrated her seventeenth birthday and certainly must have felt a special identification with that event, henceforth celebrated by the black community of Philadelphia as its own Independence Day.

Although Victor's letters do not provide details regarding his grandmother's life in Philadelphia, they do contain the following two sentences, which reveal a life of sadness and drama.

> [My grandmother] grew to be a woman and was married and went to live on a farm in the country. My mother was stolen from her in 1827 and sold into slavery at Richmond Va, and Grandmother saw her no more for 37 years.

His grandmother probably would have been married before 1812, when she would have been twenty-five years old and living away from Philadelphia, "in the country" with her husband. The year 1812 marked the beginning of a frightening new age of terror for the black population of Philadelphia and its surrounding regions, and would ultimately have a tragic impact on Victor's grandmother and her new family. The economic situation for blacks declined with the onset of the Industrial Revolution and the reopening of new trade routes with Europe after the War of 1812, both of which led to dramatic increases in foreign demand for American cotton, tobacco, rice, and other staple crops. America's agricultural South thus needed a larger labor force to work in the plantations that produced these crops. Because more and more states were passing laws prohibiting the import of slaves from Africa, plantation owners found other ways to maintain their slave population. They found their solution in the Fugitive Slave Act of 1793, which allowed owners of runaway slaves to pursue and retrieve their property without a warrant.

While more slave labor was needed in the South, new job opportunities were opening up in the industrial cities of the North. These jobs, however, were reserved for whites, including newly arrived white European immigrants. In Philadelphia as in other northern cities, the Industrial Revolution opened new doors of opportunity to whites but slammed them firmly shut to black workers. There was no

Pennsylvania Hall, built as a meeting place for abolitionists at 6th Street and Franklin Square, Philadelphia, being stormed by a mob and burned down in May 1838, soon after it opened

way for blacks to express their frustration; they were sinking deeper into poverty, and finding themselves victims of violence by white residents. During the 1820s and 1830s, there were violent attacks against blacks in Philadelphia, New York, and other cities. As many as five hundred people were engaged in one street fight in Philadelphia. One three-day riot saw the homes of thirty-one black residents destroyed, one man killed, and three black churches burned to the ground.[14]

At this same time, armed white men from the South began showing up in northern ports, ostensibly to seize what they claimed to be rightfully theirs. In reality, many free black people were caught up in this new reign of terror by southern slave owners and their surrogates in the North. Abductions of free black people went on openly, with no great outcry from the white population. At the same time, however, there were some voices of reason calling for an end to these abductions. Newspapers in Philadelphia regularly carried stories of vicious cases of kidnappings in that city and in neighboring counties, as well as in the nearby states of Maryland, Delaware, and New Jersey. The most vulnerable to these kidnapping attempts were children, who were often snatched from the streets while at play.

Philadelphia Mayor Joseph Watson took on the issue of the kidnapping of free blacks, especially children, as a personal crusade. As incidents of abduction were reported to him by the PAS and others, Mayor Watson used the city's resources to help bring the perpetrators to justice. He contacted authorities in the South, even those in strongly pro-slavery states such as Mississippi and Louisiana, who on many occasions responded respectfully to his pleas for help in returning kidnapped free black people to their homes. There was a consensus among many of these southern authorities that abducting free people was an abhorrent crime and must be thwarted at all costs.[15] There did not seem to be any evidence of similar cooperation with Mayor Watson by authorities in Virginia, however.

Victor's grandparents must have been concerned about the racial unrest in Philadelphia and about the increasing incidents of kidnappings there as well as "in the country" where they now lived. Information gleaned in the later stages of my research indicated that this place in the countryside was actually the town of Smyrna, Delaware, not far from Philadelphia. Because Smyrna then served as the central shipment point for agricultural goods, Victor's grandfather would easily have found work there. Although the overwhelming majority of African-Americans in Delaware were free, that state's legislature had passed numerous laws restricting the activities of and opportunities for black people. For example, there were few schools available for black children, and in 1826 a law was passed requiring free African-Americans to carry identity papers at all times, signed by an authorized white person. It was illegal for more than twelve blacks to gather past ten at night in winter without three "respectable" whites present.[16] All free black persons, as well as slaves, lived in constant fear of being abducted by slave-catching gangs, such as that run by the Cannon-Johnson family.

Given the time and location of Victor's mother's abduction, she could well have been a victim of this gang, led by the notorious Lucretia (Patty) Cannon. A strong, imposing red-haired woman who claimed that she could wrestle any man to the ground, Patty Cannon hired black and white accomplices who operated in Delaware, Philadelphia, and southern New Jersey. The kidnapping ring had a regular chain of posts between Philadelphia and Louisiana for the sale of kidnapped blacks. Once victims were seized, they were taken to Cannon's home and shackled in the attic, known as her "nigger keep," with its blood-soaked door and iron rings on the walls. The Cannon-Johnson gang, long targeted by Philadelphia's Mayor Watson, evaded capture for many years. The gang had two homes in the heavily wooded sections in the region of the Pennsylvania/ Maryland/Delaware border, near the Nanticoke River, which empties into the Chesapeake Bay. Patty Cannon's house sat squarely on the border between Maryland and Delaware, so that when authorities from one state came to apprehend her, she could move to a part of the house that was beyond their jurisdiction.

Patty Cannon was finally apprehended in 1829 for murder, not for kidnapping, and the gang's operations continued after her demise. She had been implicated in the murder of a Georgia slave trader who refused to pay the amount the gang had demanded. She was also indicted for the murder of an infant and two children. The black infant had been born to a slave mother owned by Patty, who feared that the father was a member of the Cannon-Johnson family. One of the two black children killed by Patty was a five-year-old girl who so annoyed Patty with her crying that she beat the child, held her face in the fire, and burned her to death. The night before Patty Cannon was scheduled to hang, someone managed to smuggle poison into her cell, and she took her own life. Before she died, another inmate overheard her confess to a priest that she had murdered eleven people, including her husband and one of her own children. She also confessed to being an accomplice in the deaths of twelve other people.[17]

Because slave-catchers like the Cannon-Johnson gang often had quotas to fill, their victims were usually placed in holding areas for weeks, or even months, until the quota was reached. Sometimes the slave ship itself, moored offshore, served this purpose. More often, the victims were kept in attics or basements. One woman, who had been a victim of kidnapping, recalled being chained in a garret and seeing two small girls chained at the other end of the room. They were later joined by more children. After about six months, they were all marched several miles before being taken in small boats out to a larger ship in the Chesapeake Bay.[18] Another former victim recalled waiting to be taken onto a boat with other slaves and seeing a little girl standing there, holding tightly to a tiny bag. The child did not cry, but her eyes filled with tears as she was forced into the boat. In reading this sad account, I could visualize Victor's mother as that little girl.

Late in my research, when I was looking for information about Victor Chambers's life in Rhode Island, I was intrigued by references in his letters to a man named Joseph H. Banks, who was living in Providence in the late 1800s and whom Victor described as his uncle. I wondered whether there was actually a family relationship or merely a loose bond based on the friendship between Mr. Banks and Victor's mother, who had once been slaves on the same plantation in Virginia. Mr. Banks's death certificate listed his wife's name as

Henrietta Chambers, born in Smyrna, Delaware, in 1828. This strongly suggested that there was indeed a familial relationship and, more importantly, that Henrietta Chambers Banks must have been the sister of Victor's mother. Henrietta was born the year after her sister had been kidnapped. The impact of losing one child in such a violent manner and giving birth to another within a year or less was just another in a series of occurrences that would have an indelible impact on the woman who had come to America from Haiti as a girl of six; who had seen so many changes as she grew up, married, and moved away from the security of her parents' home; and who would experience many more frightful and amazing events in her ninety-seven years of life.

"I tremble for my country"

I tremble for my country, when I reflect that
God is just; that his justice cannot sleep forever.
—*Thomas Jefferson*

After her abduction, Victor's mother was taken to Virginia, where she was sold at a slave auction in Richmond. Victor's letter states:

> [She was] sold in the slave markets of Richmond Va. She was bought by a planter down James River at City Point, who was the uncle of General Barksdale, who was killed . . . at Gettysburg, July 2nd 1863.

In myriad ways, Virginia gentlemen planters modeled their way of life after that of the English gentry. They also adhered to laws and exhibited attitudes toward slavery that were similar to those of their English forebears. The attitude of Virginia slave owners such as Thomas Jefferson that African-born people were somehow less human than Caucasians echoed earlier English views toward African-born slaves in their colonies.

In 1687, the English were debating whether to give slaves in Barbados the same rights extended to English subjects, specifically whether to grant slaves legal recourse for punishment by their English masters. After a short-lived debate, English lawmakers concurred that slaves did not merit equal rights under the law, on the ground that "Negroes . . . are punishable in a different and more severe manner than other Subjects." These English legislators concluded that "Negroes . . . , by means of their numbers, . . . become dangerous, and, being a brutish sort of people,. . . (must be) reckoned as goods and chattel." It was therefore necessary for their masters "to have Laws . . . to prevent the great mischief" these slaves might cause.[1]

The Commonwealth of Virginia later passed similar laws, but it went even further in providing plantation owners legal protection for themselves and the right to use force to exert leverage over their slaves. One such legal measure, entitled the "Act about the Killing of Slaves," granted Virginia's slave owners legal protection if they inadvertently killed a slave in the process of punishing him or her. This act read: "Be it enacted and declared by this grand assembly, if any slave resist his master . . . and by the extremity of the correction should chance to die, . . . his death shall not be accompted Felony, but the master (or that person appointed by the master to punish him) be acquit from molestation, since it cannot be presumed that prepensed malice should induce any man to destroy his own estate."[2]

A later amendment to this act, which was tacked on the door of every church in Virginia, dealt with the punishment of runaway slaves. It stipulated that if runaways did not turn themselves in, "it would be lawful for any person . . . to kill and destroy such slaves. If the slave were captured alive, the owner could apply to the county court "to order such punishment to the said slave, either by dismembering [sic], or any other way, not touching his life . . . as they see fit, for the reclaiming of any such incorrigible slave, and terrifying others from the like practice."[3] In practice, not many owners waited to apply to the courts in order to carry out such punishments. This, then, was the dreadful atmosphere in which Victor's mother and other victims found themselves.

The famed Civil War diarist Mary Chesnut, who was from a wealthy slave-owning family in South Carolina, stated, "God help us, but ours is a monstrous system." Yet, at the same time, she believed that slaves were for the most part "hard, unpleasant, unromantic, undeveloped, savage Africans."[4] A young woman named Letitia

Burwell, who grew up on a Virginia plantation, proudly proclaimed that her parents never abused their slaves, on the grounds that they were valuable pieces of property. "What man would pay a thousand dollars for a piece of property, and fail to take the best possible care of it?" asked Ms. Burwell, who claimed that she "never saw a discontented face" among her family's slaves.[5]

One reason that so many white slave owners maintained this mode of denial is that their whole livelihood was based on the maintenance of the slave system. The viability of the genteel and gracious lifestyle of Virginia planters—among them Washington, Jefferson, Madison, and Monroe—depended on a productive slave force that afforded their masters the time and resources to indulge in literature, philosophy, and good food and wine, as well as local and national politics. Slaves were a criterion of wealth. Many planters had no qualms about putting pregnant women or children to work in the fields. Mothers had to continue working while raising their children, and these children could, in turn, be sold at any time for profit to states farther south.

Despite the fact that the men who drafted the Constitution and the Declaration of Independence admired the English philosophers identified with the Enlightenment (or the Age of Reason, as Thomas Paine called it) and that the Declaration of Independence reflected the theories of David Hume and John Locke that the natural law guaranteed all men the right to life, liberty, and property, the reality of American life to a great extent ran counter to these ideals. A segment of the correspondence between George Washington and the Marquis de Lafayette in 1786 reveals the equivocation of Washington on the issue of slavery. In a letter to Washington, Lafayette wrote that "nothing can justify the aristocracy of the white race or excuse slavery and the slave trade" and told Washington of his plan to purchase a plantation in Cayenne in order to conduct an experiment in the freeing of slaves. Washington wrote back from Mount Vernon that he marveled at the "benevolence of your heart, my dear Marquis" and that "your . . . purchase of an estate in the Colony of Cayenne, with a view of emancipating the slaves on it, is a generous and noble proof of your humanity." He then added, "Would to God a like spirit might diffuse itself generally in the minds of the people of this country. But I despair of it. Some petitions were presented in the Assembly . . . for the abolition of slavery, but they could scarcely obtain a reading." As for Washington himself, the idea of setting the slaves "at float at once would, I really believe, be productive of much inconvenience and mischief; but by degrees it certainly might, and assuredly ought to be affected; and that too by legislative authority."[6] Washington knew full well that the legislature—dominated by slave owners—would never approve such a radical step. Like the British slave owners in Barbados, he dreaded the "mischief" that freed slaves might cause.

Thomas Jefferson, in his *Notes on the State of Virginia*, begun in 1821, reflected this same anxiety over the idea of emancipating the slaves all at once. While he believed in some form of gradual emancipation (most likely a system in which blacks would live apart from white society—either in Africa or one of the new American territories), Jefferson rejected any attempt to force masters to free their slaves. He feared that "deep rooted prejudices" on the part of whites and "ten thousand recollections" by black slaves of abuses suffered at the hands of their masters might "divide us into parties and produce convolutions which will probably never end but in the extermination of one or the other race." While Jefferson decried the system that allowed "one half of the citizens to trample on the rights of others," he also believed that, although black people were equal "in a moral sense," they were nevertheless "inferior to whites in the endowments of both body and soul."[7] Throughout his lifetime, Jefferson could not bring himself to advocate any form of emancipation, even though other Virginia planters had granted their slaves freedom, and some had even pressured Jefferson to use his prestige and influence to bring an end to this last vestige of English colonial policy.

It was just one year after Jefferson's death in 1826 that Victor Chambers's mother was brought to the slave markets of Richmond. Any visitor to Richmond at that time might have thought that city existed for no purpose other than the buying and selling of slaves. Archival records and newspapers reveal that slave markets were to be found everywhere—public squares, Oddfellows' halls, hotels, and even churches. Public and private trading went on all over the city,

A slave auction

where large numbers of slaves were available and planters from all over the South came prepared to pay high prices. Richmond city directories usually listed from thirty to fifty people as "traders," but there were hundreds of others engaged in the slave trade as auctioneers, agents, commission merchants, or planters. In the newspapers, and on the doors of public places, were all kinds of advertisements for slaves wanted or for sale. Especially high value was placed on women considered to be good "breeders," since Virginia was a veritable "nursery" of slaves, where children were born and raised, then sold to states farther south, which paid prices anywhere from 30 to 70 percent higher than in Virginia.[8] Up until the end of the Civil War, Virginia had more slaves than any other southern state.

At the markets, the auctioneers wanted to make the slaves as attractive as possible to prospective buyers. Before they left the slave pens, or holding areas, that were located throughout the city, the slaves were allowed to wash themselves. Children were sometimes given clothes and shoes to wear and small toys or coins to hold to divert their attention and keep them from crying. Once the slaves were lined up in the auction arena, the auctioneer would try to grab the audience's attention by making jokes, interspersed with bawdy remarks about young women up for sale. As slaves mounted the block, they were closely inspected. Buyers peered at their teeth and into their eyes, and often had them stripped. While this was usually for the buyers' own lewd pleasure, the buyers also wanted to make sure the slaves bore no signs of malformation or disease, nor any scars indicating previous punishment for rebelliousness.

Slave narratives give some insights into the trauma this experience inflicted. One woman recalled how she and other children had been lined up by the "Vendu Master" at an open-air auction, while men came up to her "in the same manner as a butcher would look over a calf or lamb he was about to purchase." Although she proudly told her interviewer that she had "fetched a great sum for so young a slave," she never forgot the terror of the ordeal. In order to keep herself calm—for she would be beaten if she cried—she kept thinking back to her mother whom she would never see again, and repeated to herself over and over, "Oh, my mother, my mother![9]

As the slaves were marched away by their buyers, the men were kept in the single-file coffle formation, with ropes attached around their necks, while the women and children followed under the watchful eyes of the slave drivers. Much of their travel would be by foot. These lines from a song of the men in the coffle lines reflects their despair of seeing loved ones again:

> The way is long before me,
> And all my love's behind me;
> You'll seek me down by the old gum tree,
> But none of you will find me. . . .
> I'll think of you in the cotton fields;
> I'll pray for you when resting.
> I'll look for you in every gang,
> Like the bird that's lost her nesting. . . .
> I'll leave you a drop of my heart's own blood,
> For I won't be back tomorrow.[10]

"There is an inferior race to do the menial service"

4

If there is a society on earth where there is the most perfect equality among white men, where labor is respected and the laborer honored, it is in the southern States; and the reason is obvious: There is an inferior race to do the menial service.
—*William Barksdale to U.S. Congress*

Victor Chambers said his mother was bought by a planter "down James River at City Point, who was the uncle of General (William) Barksdale." Although Victor probably remembered his mother's mention of City Point at the time that she was bought by General Barksdale's uncle, he may have mistaken that for the location of the Barksdale plantation itself. At the time that he wrote these letters, Victor Chambers was sixty-seven years old, and time may have blurred some of his recollections of his mother's words. City Point, with its strategic location at the confluence of the James and Appomattox rivers, served mainly as a transshipment point both before and after the Civil War. Before the war, it was used to move slaves from the Richmond slave markets to plantations to the south and west. During the war, it was seized by federal troops and became an important supply depot and arsenal for Union General Ulysses S. Grant.

Historians at City Point and at the nearby Petersburg National Battlefield state that there were never any viable tobacco plantations in this part of Virginia. Furthermore, neither these historians nor a local genealogist, retired professor of history at the College of William and Mary, could find any traces of the Barksdale family living in the

City Point/Petersburg area while Victor Chambers's mother was a slave. The Barksdales, like other tobacco planters, would have moved toward the southwestern part of Virginia, where the soil was more conducive to the harvesting of tobacco. The largest tobacco plantations were located in the southwestern part of the state, specifically in the Halifax and Dinwiddie counties. One history of Halifax County refers to the sale of 410 acres of land in 1788 by one Thomas Gent to "William Barksdale of Petersburg." The same Thomas Gent sold another plantation, called Seven Oaks, to John Barksdale in 1804.[1] By the late 1820s, the Barksdale family was mostly concentrated in Halifax County. The 1860 census shows no Barksdales living at City Point; in fact there were fewer than one hundred people living in City Point at that time.

The movement of the Barksdales and other prominent families to the western part of the state paralleled an important social and economic shift in Virginia at that time. Prior to the 1820s, the Tidewater city of Williamsburg was not only the state capital and center of the state's political life, it was also home to the College of William and Mary, the center of the state's intellectual life. During the late 1820s and early 1830s, the Piedmont became more prominent than the Tidewater region, with Richmond replacing Williamsburg as the capi-

William Barksdale (1821–1863), the Confederate general known to Victor Chambers's mother as "Young Massa Will"

tal, and Jefferson's University of Virginia replacing William and Mary as the state's major center of learning.

In this lush, fertile region close to the North Carolina border, with the Blue Ridge Mountains to the west, a higher quality of tobacco could be cultivated than in the sandy, nutrient-depleted soil of the Tidewater. Planters regularly visited the Richmond slave markets to replenish the labor supply they needed. After the new slaves were shipped to City Point, they were moved—mainly on foot—to the plantations. The march of about eighty miles to the Barksdale settlements near Danville, which Victor's mother would likely have taken, covered an area that featured prominently in the last days of the Civil War. The arsenal and supply depots at City Point enabled Grant to maintain his nine-hundred-day siege of Petersburg, which eventually forced Confederate General Robert E. Lee to surrender at Appomattox. On that same day, after Richmond was taken by federal troops, Jefferson Davis and his cabinet fled to Danville, which served for about one week as the last Confederate capital.

The route probably taken by Victor's mother was one of many well-worn routes to slavery in that era. Large groups of slaves were regularly seen traveling south on Virginia's roads. In 1835, a northern visitor observed "ten Negro boys between the ages of 8 and 12, tied together at the wrists and fastened with a rope. A tall white man with a whip drove them along, stopping at a horse trough to let them drink."[2] An English traveler reported seeing a caravan of about three hundred slaves in the southwestern area of Virginia in 1834. As he recalled, "They had passed the night on the bank of the New River. . . . Some of the women were sitting on logs, others were standing. Many young children were warming themselves at bivouac fires. Close at hand were about 200 male slaves, manacled and chained together in pairs. There were nine vehicles for white persons and any slaves that could no longer endure the journey on foot." When the group prepared to cross the river, "along came a four-wheeled horse wagon with another rider, and other wagons containing the children. . . . Most of the women crossed on flatboats. The men were forced to walk in chain-gang formation across the shallow part of the water." The slave-driver proudly told the Englishman that his coffle lines covered an average of twenty-five miles a day, especially "after they had been seasoned." He added that this distance was "not excessive for these sturdy slaves," and that there were "facilities so that ailing ones could ride."[3] Young children were threatened with the whip if they could not keep up the pace. For Victor's mother, who had led a protected life as a child, this must have been extremely arduous, especially since the slaves were usually barefoot. By the time she made her final trek through the Virginia countryside some thirty-seven years later, her body and spirit would have been hardened and prepared to take on the challenge of walking almost 250 miles back to freedom.

Slaves en route from City Point to western Virginia were unaware, as they filed along, of the ironic fact that their ancestral homeland and this foreign territory were actually once joined by forces of nature. Geological studies of the region indicate that, hundreds of millions of years ago, the Piedmont had been covered by ocean waters, as attested to by fossils found in the area. Later, tectonic collisions resulted in a continental clash of such magnitude that the continent of Africa smashed against the North American land mass. One result of this shift was the formation of a long mountain range along the edge of the two landmasses (now known by the American Indian word Appalachian, meaning "never-ending"). Still later, another cataclysmic shift once again separated the two continents, a phenomenon evidenced by the rocky outcroppings found throughout this part of Virginia. No one could have predicted the cataclysmic "convolutions" (to use Jefferson's term) that would later occur when the peoples of these two continents were forced together on this once-shared land: one people as slaves, and the other as masters.

As I traveled along this route in early summer, I marveled at the beauty of the land and at the rolling ridges that seem to grow darker as they continue into the distance. If the line of slaves containing Victor's mother had made their journey at this same time of year, nature may have provided them some solace, as they trekked through the lovely countryside and as the sweet smell of honeysuckle and the soft sounds of murmuring streams permeated their senses and soothed their spirits. At the same time, they no doubt felt an increasing sense of foreboding as to what awaited them at the end of the march. As they moved toward their destination, they learned to be wary of those poisonous snakes that lay in wait for warm-blooded prey. During the hot days of summer, in particular, water moccasins and copperheads lurk in the forests and rocky ledges, ready to strike out at anything that moves.

At the time of her abduction, Victor's mother was probably not aware of the identity of the man who bought her. For generations, the Barksdale family had played a prominent role in the life of Virginia and the South. The first Barksdale to emigrate from England to Virginia was William Barksdale (born ca. 1629). Genealogists concur that he was probably the progenitor of all the Barksdales of colonial Virginia. There are few solid facts about the second generation; as one family history states, "the second generation is clouded by lack of sufficient records and data."[4] By the third generation, there were seven Barksdales, all of whom were believed to be grandsons of William.

Carrington's *History of Halifax County* describes the Barksdales as "professional and educational people [who] . . . have always been prominent in Halifax County. They have been considerable land and slave owners, and their influence in politics and religion is well established. . . . The family is extensive by virtue of intermarriage with many of the leading people of the county and the kinship, though interesting, is difficult when it comes to connecting the various lines."[5] Even John Augustus Barksdale, who wrote a family history and genealogy in 1940, was unable to connect the lines within the earlier generations.

One grandson of the original William, also named William, had a son, Nathaniel (b. 1707), who eventually moved from the Tidewater to Halifax County, where he built up a large estate and tobacco plantation. In 1808, Nathaniel's grandson William moved his family to Smyrna, Tennessee, near Nashville. This William in turn had four sons who, after his death, moved to Mississippi to seek their fortunes.[6] One of these sons became the Confederate General William Barksdale (b. 1821, d. 1863), known to Victor's mother as "young Massa Will."

Henry Barksdale (b. 1710), probably a first cousin of Nathaniel, also left the Tidewater for Halifax County. One of his four sons, named Beverly (1756–1822), became the largest planter of all the Barksdales.[7] His son, Colonel Beverly Barksdale, inherited the plantation after his father's death and expanded its facilities. While it is impossible to know which Barksdale had bought Victor's mother (especially since the slave schedules for Halifax county, most signed by a local lawyer named Barksdale, identify slaves only by sex, approximate age, and color), the most likely owner would have been Colonel Beverly Barksdale, who had a large number of slaves divided among himself and his children and was probably a regular client of the Richmond slave markets. Even if he was not the owner of this particular slave, so much has been recorded about him in local histories and genealogies that a review of his life provides useful insights into how the planters of the region thought and operated, and how their slaves may have lived. Although Victor Chambers described his mother's owner as an uncle of the future General William Barksdale, the exact relationship between the general and his Virginia relatives was more probably one of younger cousin to older cousins.[8]

Like many of the Barksdales, the elder Beverly had a strong, willful nature. He left home at the age of fourteen after his father gave him a severe beating, and he earned his own living from then on. At first he delivered goods by wagon between Richmond and the western counties; during the Revolutionary War he hauled military supplies between Richmond and South Carolina; he also operated a country store. Upon his marriage to Anna Terry around 1782, Beverly's future father-in-law loaned his daughter two male slaves. Aware of the status and prestige associated with owning one's own slaves, Beverly immediately returned the two slaves to Mr. Terry, with a terse note stating that he "wanted no borrowed Negroes."[9]

After Anna's death around 1789, Beverly moved to the extreme southwestern part of Halifax County, becoming the first Barksdale to buy land in that part of the state. Here he amassed a huge fortune and certainly had no need for borrowed slaves. In 1801 he married Judith Womack of Halifax County. Beverly's estate and holdings, named Brooklyn, covered several hundred acres on land extending from the Dan River to an area near New Boston. After his death, his son, Colonel Beverly Barksdale, made several additions. Some local records estimated the Brooklyn tract at 438 acres, and the elder Barksdale had other substantial holdings. This is evident in his will, dated April 22, 1822, in which he divided his properties among his seven children: "To Claiborne . . . the land on Dan River called Boyd's Tract, containing 267 acres; to Elizabeth . . . my tract of land on Dan River; to Henry . . . my Mill Tract; to John . . . the tract of land on which I now reside; to Maryann . . . my tract of land on Wolf Hill Creek; to Martha . . . the Dodson tract." His widow received other land, with the stipulation that, should she marry again, it would be reduced by one-third. Still other land was to be sold and applied to the elder Beverly's debts. The younger Beverly inherited the Brooklyn tract.[10]

On most plantations in this area, slaves were scattered about the land, organized in clusters of simple cabins close to their work. Slaves who worked as domestics in the main house were usually assigned to quarters set apart from, but close to, the house. Also near the main house were service buildings and workshops for slaves such as carpenters, coopers, shoemakers, and washerwomen. Masters grouped their slaves for control directly by themselves or by overseers. Slave cabins were usually arranged in rows, facing directly onto a road or

The main house at Brooklyn, on the Barksdale plantation

aligned to it, so that masters or overseers could easily observe their movements. This clustering actually had the effect of providing the slaves with a means of constant interaction and mutual support. The practice of aligning slave cabins with the main house at the head of the row inadvertently followed an African site-planning tradition in which the chief's residence had a dominant position.[11] Some slave areas had room for small garden plots or even space for poultry and pigs, so that slaves could supplement their meager rations. In good weather, outdoor spaces between the cabins could be used as extra "rooms" where food preparation and child care could take place.

It was especially important for plantations to be close to water routes that could be used to transport tobacco and other products. The Brooklyn site met this criterion. It also boasted a store that carried a line of silk and other luxury fabrics comparable to that available in cities. The store also housed the Brooklyn post office. At first, mail arrived by horse-drawn wagon, but it later came by train to nearby Barksdale's Depot (named for other Barksdale settlers in the county), and was brought to Brooklyn by rider.

Beverly Barksdale had goods shipped from Baltimore to North Carolina, then by river to nearby Milton, to be hauled overland from there by slaves to Brooklyn for sale in his store. He and a partner also built a tobacco factory on the property in 1855; it operated for almost a century, with the exception of the Civil War, when it was closed. Both the store and the tobacco factory are still standing. Old ledgers from the Barksdale store show that buyers came from as far as Baltimore and Philadelphia to purchase luxury goods.

The main house at Brooklyn still stands and was restored in the late 1990s. It was sold by Ruth and Elizabeth Barksdale, elderly sisters, in 1972. Many of the old trees and shrubs were gone, but new boxwood has been planted to restore the former boxwood avenue leading to the graceful home. Not far behind the main house is a small family burial plot, where generations of Barksdales, including Beverly Barksdale, are buried. In 1937, the Works Progress Administration of Virginia's Historical Inventory carried this description:

This is an attractive home located about 30 yards from the highway (now route 659). The yard is enclosed with palings. The dwarf boxwood on each side of the walk is as high as the fence and extends from the front gate almost to the porch where there are two large box trees, one on each side. . . . The front windows on the second floor are arched. The entrance to the reception hall has one door with side lights and lights over the door. The stairway is in this hall. On the left is the parlor, on the right is a bedroom and at the back of the hall is the dining room, which is about two feet lower than the hall with steps leading down to it. The rooms are large and high pitched.[12]

Victor Chambers said that his mother was "well acquainted with young Massa Will," who may have visited his uncle's plantation fairly frequently when his family was living in Tennessee. If the man reflects the boy he once was, young Will would have been noted for his ability to race horses faster than anyone, perhaps with reckless abandon, his hair blowing wildly in the wind just as it did when he led his troops at Gettysburg, with his white wispy hair blowing about like a plume.[13] After reading accounts of eulogies made after his death, and the value that others placed on his friendship, I can imagine that other children vied to be admitted to his valued circle of friends, while few, if any, could match his speed, daring, and strength. But young Will Barksdale was unaware that on his uncle's plantation there was one child, about the same age as himself, who could equal him in strength of character, bravery, and determination. She would also be one day at Gettysburg, and her son would be born near the spot where Will Barksdale would lead his last charge.

"Man is slave only to himself"

5

> We have known bondage, . . .
> We have known pain and humiliation.
> But man is slave only to himself . . .
> —*Quoted in Pauli Murray, Slave Testimony*

Once she had entered into the abyss of slavery in 1827, nothing more is known of Victor Chambers's mother until her escape thirty-seven years later. Just how she was treated, and how much of this she shared with her son, will never be known. For years, as I read and reread Victor's letters, I kept wondering: Were slave children on the plantation resentful of this girl, who was born into a different kind of environment and was used to different kinds of clothes and food? Was she a domestic slave, or did she work in the tobacco fields? What were her owners like? Were they "benevolent," or did they mistreat her? Was she sexually abused and exploited by her owner, as many women were? Did she ever experience love, or develop friendships with young men her age? Did she have any other children? If so, did they remain on the plantation, or were they sold to other plantations, or other states? If she did have other children, was the father the same person? Was that person her owner? What did Victor mean when he said that she "was well acquainted with young Massa Will"? Did Victor really know what the relationship was? Was her escape in 1863 her first such attempt? Did she ever lose faith in God, or despair of ever seeing her parents again?

While none of these questions can be answered, some insights into how she lived during these long years as a slave can be found in the vast archives and records of slave narratives and interviews that offer a compelling view into the slave system as a whole. While the Barksdales may have been fairly "benevolent" masters who did not engage in the abuse described in so many slave narratives, the undeniable fact remains that Victor's mother was a slave and the victim of a system in which she and others were reduced to less than human status and denied all freedom of choice.

Although many slave interviews were embellished by the abolitionists who compiled them, and although those conducted in the 1930s under the aegis of the Works Progress Administration (WPA) were done when the former slaves were very elderly (in their eighties and nineties), their impact and import does not suffer from that. They all touch on the same basic themes, providing strikingly similar insights into issues such as relationships among the slaves themselves, relations with masters and overseers, the role of religion, forms of slave resistance, and the dangers of escape. The embellishments within interviews conducted by abolitionists during and after the Civil War are easy to detect, usually taking the form of preachy sermonizing clumsily inserted into the text. But the voices that speak to us from the depths of slavery do not need these artificial touches to affect us; they speak with passion, truth, and authenticity. Despite the great age of those interviewed by WPA writers in the 1930s, the former slaves had remarkably fresh and detailed recollections of events that occurred in their childhood years. An elderly woman exclaimed to a WPA interviewer, "Oh God! I can feel the torment now—the terrible agony of those moments!"[1]

Another former slave remembered how, after having been kidnapped as a child and sent to a large plantation, she was first brought to the slave quarters. When two women there asked who she was, she responded, "I am come to live here." The reply was, "Poor child, poor child! You must have a good heart if you are to live here." When the little girl started to cry, one of the women said, "You are not come here to stand in a corner and cry; you are come here to work." She was forced to clean and wash the floors and the rest of the cabin. Soon thereafter, she was assigned domestic duties in the main house.

Because she was not used to such heavy work, she tired easily; as a result, she was beaten severely with a cow-skin belt and forced to stand up all night at a bench, washing laundry in scalding hot water. She was not allowed to drop down from fatigue; if she did, she would receive more beatings.[2]

Northern abolitionists visiting the South in the 1850s were struck by a song they heard slave children singing. While the words might shock us today, they reveal the deep impact that separation from their mothers had on their psyche:

> I wonder where my mother's gone.
> Sing, Oh graveyard!
> I wonder where my mother's gone.
> Graveyard ought to know.[3]

Mothers also looked to the comforting words of hymns for consolation, especially distressed mothers separated from their children. Many such women found expression for their grief in the old Methodist hymn:

> Good bye, I'm going to leave you,
> Good bye, I'll meet you in the kingdom.[4]

In recalling his childhood on a plantation in the Virginia Piedmont, Booker T. Washington said that there was never any period solely devoted to play. "Almost every day of my life (was) . . . occupied in some kind of labor."[5] He described the slave cabins: The only "windows" were openings cut into the side to let in light, and the cold air of winter as well. The "doors" were crude pieces of wood covered with cracks and holes that only added to the over-

Booker T. Washington

all discomfort of the place. The "floor" was just bare earth. In the center was usually a large, deep opening covered with boards, which was used for storing root vegetables in the winter. All the cooking was done on an open fireplace. No one had beds to sleep on; everyone slept on a pallet, or, rather, "a bundle of filthy rags" laid upon the dirt floor. Other slaves who lived in this general area of southwestern Virginia told of living in huts where the roofs constantly leaked in the rain, making the dirt floor soiled and muddy. No slaves had blankets, even in the cold Virginia winters when snow and ice would fall through to the frozen dirt floor of the cabin.[6]

On a thriving tobacco plantation, there was a wide variety of tasks for all the slaves, including children. In addition to cultivating and harvesting the tobacco, slaves were responsible for other tasks such as making barrels, packing tobacco leaves, tending to horses and other domestic animals, handling shipments at the docks, building and repairing roads, bridges, and ditches, cutting timber, making and laying bricks, milling grain, and processing other crops grown on the plantation. There was also a wide variety of domestic tasks, including work as grooms, teamsters, blacksmiths, and coachmen. Slaves had to cook, churn butter, wash and mend clothing and linens, weave cloth, and mend shoes.

Successful planters such as Beverly Barksdale knew that, to be skilled and productive workers, slaves needed expert training and constant supervision. The role of overseer was thus of great importance. Also, the more overseers on a plantation, the more time the planter had for leisurely pursuits. It was not just by chance that tobacco crops thrived as they did in Virginia. Tobacco is a very difficult crop to cultivate, and the survival of this crop depended on a well-trained and carefully supervised slave labor force.

The plants must be started as seedlings, then carefully transplanted into uniform-shaped mounds of soil and manure. The seedlings and young plants require conscientious monitoring. Since there were no modern pesticides, each plant had to be inspected by hand for pests or disease; plants also had to be carefully pruned so that growth would be concentrated into the broad lower leaves. Throughout the processes of harvesting, curing, and packing, workers had to take

great care not to tear or bruise the sensitive leaves. Severe and immediate punishment would befall any slave who fell short in performing
these duties.

The tobacco plants were set out in spring, after slaves had cleared
and prepared the soil. In order to keep worms away from the succu-
lent leaves, small slave children were trained to pull worms away
from the plants and kill them. A child who missed any worms would
have to eat them and/or be beaten. On her first day at this task, one
five-year old girl missed some worms. The overseer immediately
picked up a handful of worms and stuffed them into her mouth. He
stood over her and made sure she swallowed them all before she was
returned to her place in the field.[7]

During the midsummer harvest, slaves would receive lashings if
they cut any leaves before they were ripe. Women were assigned the
task of tying the leaves together and letting them cure, or smoke, in
the barn. Children were often assigned to make sure the fires did not
go out during the two-day and two-night curing period, no matter
what the weather was like. If the fires did go out, the tobacco would
be spoiled and the planter would suffer a monetary loss. The punishment for this would be particularly severe.

Most owners believed that systematic disciplining of child slaves
was necessary "to make them subdue." This somehow enabled owners to rationalize brutal beatings, denial of food, and other means to
bring the young slaves to submission. Virginia planters regularly read
issues of *The Southern Planter* to obtain useful information about the
cultivation of crops, as well as the proper handling of livestock and
slaves (in that order). An 1852 issue contained an article by one W.
W. Gilmer, who described desirable behavior for young slaves. "Tell
them to stand their ground, and speak when spoken to, in a polite
manner."[8] A former slave described what this entailed: "We were . . .
drilled in the art of addressing (our owners and visitors). The boys
were required to bend the body forward, with the weight of the body
on the left foot, and scrape the right foot backward on the ground,
while uttering the words 'How dy Massie and Missie.'" Girls were
taught to curtsy while repeating the same words.[9]

Even though they were treated as harshly as the adults, slave children were often better fed to keep them healthy and help them grow into strong, productive adult slaves. Owners were often alarmed at the rates of sickness and death among the slave population. In Prince George County, Virginia, twenty-nine out of forty-six slave infants born at the Beechwood Plantation between 1803 and 1829 died. Between 1839 and 1849, eighteen out of thirty-nine infants there died. Other plantations showed similar mortality rates for infants.[10]

Many babies born to slaves died natural deaths due to inadequate shelter, nutrition, or care; to suffocation caused by sleeping in the same bed as exhausted mothers; or to what we would now refer to as Sudden Infant Death Syndrome.[11] On the other hand, we will never know how many cases of infant deaths were caused by oppressed and hopeless mothers who chose to kill their own babies, believing that they would be happier in heaven than during a lifetime of slavery.

Overall mortality rates remained high for slaves, due to mistreatment, malnutrition, and disease. This is clearly illustrated in the antebellum mortality rates for one Virginia region:[12]

Year	Whites	Slaves
1850	111	178
1853	111	172
1855	105	151
1857	97	152
1858	95	146

Many slaves from the southern Virginia plantations said that they never sat down to have a meal all the time that they were slaves. Children got food much as animals did—a piece of bread here, a scrap of meat there, sometimes a potato or small cup of milk. Food rations were given out on most plantations on Saturday night. This sometimes consisted of cornmeal, lard, molasses, greens, and flour. One plantation in northern Virginia gave each household of slaves a peck of sifted cornmeal, a dozen herrings, and two pounds of pork products (usually chitterlings). Those owners who allowed slaves to raise their own vegetables and poultry were in the minority. Most slaves saw meat less than six times a year; the main staples were corn, and, occasionally, buttermilk. Owners did not want to see slaves "wasting their time eating" when they could be working productively in the fields. The main daily meal was usually a hoecake: corn ground to a coarse meal and prepared in the field. The slaves would build a fire and roast the cakes on their hoe blades. Often before everyone could reach the fire to cook their cakes, the overseer's horn would sound, and the slaves had to return to the field, with some never getting a chance to eat.

Just as inadequate as the food was the type of clothing available to slaves. Booker T. Washington described the shirt he was forced to wear as a child. It was made of flax—or rather, the cheapest and roughest part of the fiber. "I can scarcely imagine any torture, except for the pulling of a tooth, that is equal to that caused by putting on a new flax shirt for the first time. . . . . [It was] like having a dozen chestnut burrs, or a hundred small pinpoints, in contact with the flesh."[13]

For young children, especially those who were cruelly separated from their families, there was one consolation. Older women were usually asked to supervise the slave children while their mothers and other young adults worked in the field. The women and children often bonded, developing a community spirit that served as a buffer against a depersonalizing system. The female community made sure that no child was truly motherless, and it was thanks to the efforts of older slave women that many young girls in particular developed a sense of self-respect and self-worth. Former slave Lucy Delaney said that her mother and other slave women instilled in her a hope of freedom and pride in themselves. These women were living role models who would not give in to despair. Lucy said that, when told later in life by her mistress that she should accept slavery "with submission and patience," she rejected that concept, stating, "I could not feel anything but rebellion against my lot."[14] Another woman said that no matter how terrible the agony, "I did not scream; I was too proud to let my tormentor know what I was suffering."[15] This passive resistance and refusal to let their oppressors know what they were feeling was one of the few defensive weapons that slave women could use.

Families were often separated, and slaves were not allowed to develop any close affections or ties. As a result, slaves learned to hide their emotions and thoughts and dared not reveal their intelligence openly. To achieve this, they had to mask their true feelings. Letitia Burwell, who "never saw a discontented face" among her family's slaves, was not aware of what was going on behind the masks being shown to her.

Secrecy and guile became important weapons of defense for slaves and would later help them evade capture when fleeing from their oppressors. Even though slaves were not allowed to become educated—especially after the insurrection led by Nat Turner in 1831—some had clandestine ways of learning. Some created "pit schools" run by fellow slaves, free blacks, or white abolitionists. These were located in holes dug large enough for two to four people and covered with brush to conceal the participants. Down in the pit, slaves and their teachers practiced their lessons with less chance of being caught. It was very dangerous, because, if caught, slaves would be sent to the Deep South, where any chance of escape was even more remote than in Virginia. Religious services represented an opportunity for slaves to express their emotions and their desire for freedom. Although the word "freedom" could not be uttered openly, slaves found its meaning in the words of hymns and spirituals. Slaves used every prayer as a petition for escape and freedom, and looked forward to religious music sessions on Sunday evenings and general prayer meetings on Wednesday nights.

Frederick Douglass said that the song "Run to Jesus" was the inspiration for his escape from slavery. As a young boy, he loved to hear the slaves sing this song, which was sung with greatest enthusiasm when they reached the words "I don't expect to stay much longer here."

> Run to Jesus, shun the danger!
> I don't expect to stay much longer here![16]

At the time of the Nat Turner insurrection, owners tightened controls over their slaves. Victor's mother, who would have been about nine years old at the time, must have felt the effect of these restrictions. Turner's failed rebellion threatened to overthrow the institu-

tion of slavery in Southampton County, Virginia, and its repercus-
sions were felt throughout Virginia and the rest of the slaveholding
South. For weeks and months after Turner's execution, there were
rumors of planned violent slave revolts elsewhere. Plantation owners
feared large-scale rebellions similar to those that had occurred in
Saint Domingue in the 1790s, although the conditions for any successful revolt were not present in the American South. Here, slaves
were neither armed nor able to organize, because of the close control
and surveillance of overseers and masters. Nevertheless, owners and
overseers increased their vigilance, and bands of white men stepped
up patrols in the towns, attacking and harassing even free black residents without cause.

After the Nat Turner uprising, laws were quickly passed in Virginia
forbidding slaves from holding religious services without permission.
If caught doing so, the penalty would be thirty-nine lashes. To prevent religious services from becoming occasions to foment slave
uprisings, more laws were passed requiring the presence of "appropriate white ministers" and other white men to supervise the services.[17] Slave owners often attended as well. Using religion as a means
to exert control over the slaves, the carefully selected preachers
stressed the importance of serving the master and mistress, citing
such Bible passages as "Obey your master." The white minister of the
First African Church in Richmond told his black congregation, "God
has given this country to the white people. They are the lawmakers—
the masters—the superiors. The people of color are the subjects—the
servants—and, even when not in bondage, the inferiors. In this state
of things, God enjoins you to your submission."[18]

Despite these constraints, slaves created what some called "hush
harbors," or secret places in the nearby forests where they could pray
and sing the hymns of freedom. Hush harbors also served often as
starting points for escape. If a slave betrayed these secret prayer meetings to the master, all would be savagely beaten. Despite efforts by
whites to suppress their religious fervor, slaves and free blacks continued to express their deep spiritual desires in prayer.

Like other southern pastoral associations, the Dan River
Association, whose jurisdiction included the Barksdale plantation,

met regularly to discuss ways in which religion could be presented to slaves. The minutes of one 1857 session showed some evolution in the pastors' approach. These read: "With God there is no respect of persons. Christ died for slaves as well as the master." To assuage any concerns by their white brethren, the churchmen added the following instructions: "Slaves must be taught religion at home, by heads of families, both by precept and example. . . . There must be plain preaching to the Negro at frequent or stated periods."[19] This latter wording left much to the individual owner's imagination and discernment.

In addition to using religion as a form of control, slave owners also exerted psychological control. Some believed that Nat Turner had only used his education as a means of revenge. Owners wanted to see slaves as ignorant and superstitious, and slaves in turn often chose to reinforce the image of childlike and gullible people both to avoid punishment and to fool the masters. Ghost tales were encouraged and fabricated to keep slaves from circulating at night. Owners spread tales of beasts who made unearthly sounds and of fearful creatures such as headless riders who appeared at night. Men who participated as "night riders" along roads next to the slave quarters would use disguises, noisemakers, and other props to frighten the slaves. Masters spread the word that certain roads and trails were haunted, and some wore sheets, masqueraded as ghosts. This ploy was later adopted by Ku Klux Klan members, who also wore sheets to reinforce belief in their supernatural powers.

There was an event in 1833 that did amaze and frighten many slaves and others in the mid-Atlantic region. It was not an invention staged by men, but rather a phenomenon of nature. On November 12, 1833—when Victor's mother would have been eleven or twelve years old—residents of Virginia witnessed a veritable shower of stars falling from the skies during the night. There was real panic in some areas, with many believing that doomsday had arrived. For some slaves, it may have called to mind the old hymn:

> Stars and the elements are falling,
> The moon in blood drips away.
> Yonder the Angel is calling
> The sheep in the fold this day.[20]

Because of its great impact, the celestial event was recorded in the histories of several Virginia counties. One history of Prince George County noted that the first of the "shooting stars" appeared just before midnight. Hundreds of others fell in increasing numbers until their light "eclipsed the rays of the rising sun." Boatmen and slaves working on the James River docks at City Point were terrified by what appeared to be "swords, scythes and reap hooks in the sky."[21] The young Frederick Douglass, who saw the same meteor shower from his plantation on the Wye River in Delaware, was "awestruck" at the unusually brilliant display, and thought it might be "a harbinger of the coming of the Son of Man."[22]

Victor Chambers's mother may have remembered this night years later as she watched the battle at Gettysburg from a protected hiding place, watching the swords and bayonets gleaming in the sun, and shells bursting in the air like stars falling from the sky onto the weary men below.

Slaves who had originally come from Dahomey or other West African regions might have seen this large number of falling stars as souls of the dead returning to the land of their ancestors. The Dahomeans believed that the sight of a star falling into the sea during or after a burial ceremony indicated that the spirit of the deceased had completed its journey, since it is through the sea that the spirit makes its way to the land of the dead.[23]

What people saw in November 1833 was the Leonid meteor shower, which is usually visible at that time of year. The Leonids hit the earth's atmosphere faster than others; the debris stream from the main comet contains significant numbers of large meteorites. Although most fragment in the upper atmosphere, others are large enough to produce fireballs when they hit the lower atmosphere. Some people claim to hear swooshing sounds as the stars fall. Scientists report that sometimes, if a fireball penetrates to a certain level, it can even produce sonic booms. Even though we now know more about these phenomena and can predict when then will occur, they still evoke reactions of wonder, and people react much as they did in 1833. NASA reported that the 1996 Leonid storm produced tens of thousands of shooting stars per hour, compared to five hundred per hour in 1998 and 2001. In describing what they had seen, eyewitnesses used words such as "spectacular . . . unearthly . . . unforgettable . . . like a blizzard of stars" or even "like the world coming to an end." Witnesses to the 1998 shower in Hong Kong and other areas in East Asia described fireballs and shooting stars of great magnitude, some so bright they cast shadows. Pictures taken from a Chinese observatory in 1998 showed forms which resembled swords or scythes, as seen in 1833.[24]

For those who thought the meteor storm of 1833 foretold the end of their days as slaves, their hopes and expectations were dashed and extinguished as swiftly as the stars falling from the sky on that November night. Victor Chambers's mother would have to endure another quarter-century of deprivation and despair before her hopes of freedom would at last be realized. One day she would also look to the stars in night sky for guidance and direction northward in her arduous nocturnal march toward freedom.

6 | "She is rising"

Even at the tomb there is hope, for she is rising. She is out there already, bearing her alabaster jar of hope. She is shaking off the old names and claiming names of her own. She is uttering truths long ago stored away. . . . She is rising, and she is good!. . . She is the Father and the Mother. . . . She is our hope. . . . And she is rising.
—*Macrina Wiederkehr, "Song of the Seed"*

Like the other thousands of "children of disappointment" mourned by W. E. B. DuBois, Victor's mother spent many years of her life in bondage. As she grew into adolescence and womanhood, she probably wondered if her parents and grandparents were still alive, or if they would recognize her now. The passing years would bring more disappointment for her and the other slaves who, like the ancient Israelites in the desert, lived in exile, singing their sorrow songs and yearning for a truer world beyond. For her, however, the pain was even more acute because she had once known that truer world.

As the years progressed, she must have found it increasingly difficult to recall that world, and may have wondered at times if it were all a dream. At times, she may have called out for her mother's guidance and help, only to meet with the now familiar silence, remembering that she was indeed "motherless" and alone. The words of this old spiritual seem to reflect the state of mind of slaves such as she had been for so long.

I am a motherless child . . .
Just look at the shape I'm in,
Just look at the shape I'm in . . .
I've been in the storm so long.

Even as she formed friendships with other slaves, these had to be kept within the confines and regulations of the plantation. Attempts by slaves to visit friends at nearby plantations, without the master's permission, would be met by severe floggings. To inflict the greatest amount of pain on their victims, the master or overseer would use an especially cruel type of lash, which consisted of a strip of raw hide, cut along the whole length of an ox and twisted while still moist until the strip tapered to a point. When it was dried and hardened, it had sharp edges projecting at every turn of the flesh and every stroke of the lash. This method of punishment was used on men, women, and children.[1]

If a slave did not work to the overseer's satisfaction, he or she would be immediately flogged in the field. The slave would be thrown down on the ground, with arms and legs extended to stakes driven into the ground. After receiving 150 lashes, one man was so weakened when he returned to the field that he crept away to lie

Flogging of a slave

down. The overseer, thinking the man asleep or lazy, crept up and beat him some more—but the man was already dead from the lashing. Sometimes, rather than tying the victim down on the ground, the owner or overseer would tie the person's hands behind him or her and throw the rope over a beam or tree limb. The slave's feet would then be tied together and a smaller beam placed over the legs to weigh down the body. In this way, the person would be fully stretched out and unable to flinch from the blows of the lash.[2]

Not even for pregnant women was there was any mercy or special treatment. The overseer would simply dig out the earth under the woman's belly and stretch her out on the ground, tied with stakes, so that her body would lie flat to receive the full force of the blows. After normal work hours (that is, after sunset), floggings took place in the barn or other outbuildings; here, slaves would be tied in a standing position and whipped with the lash. For a woman, this would consist of 50 to 70 lashes; for men, 100 to 200; and for any man or woman who struck back at the master or overseer, it would be 500 blows. In at least one case, a cat was tied onto a man's back while he was being whipped, so that the cat would bite and scratch the quivering flesh. In other cases, brine was poured over the open wounds.[3]

In line with existing Virginia laws which permitted a master or overseer to dismember, maim, or kill any slave who attempted to run away, punishment for such an offense was swift and severe for men and women alike. Women caught trying to escape were mutilated in many ways: having ears split; being branded on the hand, arm, leg, or stomach with a hot iron; and having one or more fingers cut off—to serve as an example to other slaves of what would happen if they tried to do the same. Any woman who refused to submit to her master's sexual desires would also be severely whipped. Even those who were well into pregnancy were not immune from rape or the lash. If the punishment was not successful and the woman continued to resist, she would be sold off to the Deep South, where Virginia slaves knew there would be no hope for escape.

A slave woman had no human value and was treated as a piece of property, like cattle. Any children she bore could be taken away at any time and sold to plantations farther south, where they would bring more profit to the master. While childbirth was a life-affirming action for many slave women, the repeated selling away of children from mothers valued only as "breeders" had a devastating effect. As Elizabeth Fox-Genovese writes, the master was able to exploit the slave women's productive as well as reproductive capabilities.[4] While men were valued for their work or productive abilities, women, on the other hand, had dual value: both as workers and as breeders able to replenish the slave labor force. Non-childbearing women would usually be sent farther south, where having productive workers was all that mattered to owners. In Virginia, a woman's ability to produce more slaves was of the greatest value. Thomas Jefferson stated in his Farm Book that "a woman who brings a child every two years [is] more profitable than the best man on the farm. . . . What she produces is an addition to the capital, while his labor disappears in mere consumption."[5]

Any woman capable of producing children regularly—usually every two and one-half years—could be assured of staying on the same plantation for many years. The fact that Victor's mother remained on the same Virginia tobacco plantation for thirty-seven years lends more credence to the likelihood that she had borne other children before her flight in 1863. Owners had no qualms about forcing slave women to keep producing children, even though childbearing in the mid-nineteenth century was fraught with risks. Just like those whites who believed black slaves had no feelings or emotions similar to their own and could thus work harder and endure severe punishments, many plantation owners believed that slave women "were not subject to the difficulty, danger and pain which attended women of the better classes in giving birth to their offspring."[6]

Slave women saw no hope for themselves or the next generation, and many gave way to depression. Some women sought to destroy their own value as property by destroying their children—especially if the child's father were the master or overseer, or if they just had seen too many of their children taken away and could not bear to see any more sold away. The deep sadness of those who never knew what became of children they had borne, or chose to destroy them before they could be taken away, is reflected in many of the American slaves' sorrow songs.

Oh! Child! Thou art a little slave
Thou art a little slave, my child,
And much I grieve and mourne
That so dark a destiny [befell]
The lovely babe I'd borne.

A master could arrange marriages between slaves for the sole purpose of producing children to work on his own plantation or for sale
to plantations farther south. Since it was the mother's race that determined the race of her children, any children fathered by the master
or overseer would be considered black, no matter what the color of
their skin. The master had free access to women held as slaves on his
property. Even though white masters freely exploited black women
sexually, they still had to be discreet in order to shield their actions
from their wives, whom they believed to be ignorant about what was
going on in the slave quarters at night.

Some slave women actually sought out relationships with their
overseers or masters in the hope of gaining special treatment for
themselves or their children—a tactic that only reinforced the image
of the black woman as a seductress. While a small percentage of slave
women fit into the two stereotypes white people formed of black
women (either a seductive "Jezebel" or a harmless, benevolent
"Mammie"), the African-American slave women survived neither as
helpless, inferior females nor as predatory temptresses. They sur-
mounted their terrible fate through supporting each other; finding
creative ways to resist and rebel against the tyranny forced on them;
and reconnecting with their African heritage, particularly the spiritual beliefs of their ancestors. Women who endured the hardship and
pain of slavery emerged as strong, deeply spiritual and courageous
persons. To make matters worse, male slaves were essentially power-
less to stop this abuse.

Enslaved men whose wives were sexually abused by masters had no
recourse or protection under the law. A man who tried to intervene
would either be sent to another plantation or, worse, summarily
hanged. There was no way to retaliate. The frustration of not being
able to protect their wives from the master's lust and anger drove

many men to flee to the North, where they hoped to obtain freedom for their wives and families. Henry Bibb, who escaped to Windsor, Ontario, wrote to his former master in 1844, "To be compelled to stand by and see you whip and slash my wife without mercy, when I could afford her no protection, not even by offering myself to suffer the lash in her place. . . . this kind of treatment was what drove me from home and family, to seek a better home for them."[7]

While owners believed their wives innocently unaware of the true nature of their relations with slave women, their wives knew the truth of the situation. Southern diarist Mary Chesnut wrote, "Like the patriarchs of old, our men live all in one house with their wives and their concubines; and the mulattos one sees in every family partly resemble the white children. Any lady is ready to tell you who is the father of all the mulatto children in everybody's household but her own. These, she seems to think, drop from the clouds!"[8]

Some mistresses, choosing to remain ignorant of their husbands' relations with slave women, actually played an enabling role in their husbands' behavior. Even when the mistress could see the resemblance to her husband in some of the slave children, she preferred not to hear or see the reality of the situation.

W. E. B. DuBois, who greatly revered and was inspired by his mother, saw the debasement of black women as one of the worst results of the slave system: "I shall forgive the South much in its final judgement day: I shall forgive its slavery . . . I shall forgive its fighting for a long-lost cause . . . I shall forgive its so-called pride of race. . . . but one thing I shall never forgive, neither in this world nor in the world to come: its wanton and continued and persistent insulting of . . . black womanhood." DuBois equally criticized "smug Northern hypocrites . . . who insist on withholding from my mother and wife and daughter the signs and appellations of courtesy and respect which elsewhere [they withhold] only from bawds and courtesans!"[9] The same indignant tone, used by Victor Chambers in describing the South, particularly Confederate soldiers ("They hated you then, they hate you now!"), likely stems from his mother's recollections and his own anger at the injustice done to her.

Slave women did not always respond passively to actions designed to take away their dignity. They engaged in collective and individual acts of rebellion and resistance to devalue the master's property or express their defiance. Their "weapons" of defense included arson, poison, pregnancy, and feigned illness, as well as abortion and infanticide. One elderly slave admitted that, as a cook, she had found many ways to exact her revenge: "How many times I spit in the biscuits and peed in the coffee just to get back at them mean white folks!"[10]

Slave women learned to depend on each other for midwifery, child care, and medicinal care. They used herbal concoctions to induce abortions; wild tansy was widely used in the South for this purpose. There were usually older women on each plantation who were knowledgeable about the African techniques of midwifery and herbalism and handed them down to selected younger women. Some of these older women had been also been trained in African spiritual beliefs and practices, including *vodou* brought from Dahomey to Haiti and ultimately to American plantations in the south.

Women trained in these traditions could prepare charms for specific purposes, such as protection from harm. Some believed they were born with the magic or charm needed to protect them throughout life. When asked how she managed to evade capture after having freed more than three hundred slaves, the deeply Christian Harriet Tubman exclaimed: "I was born with the charm, and the Lord has given me the power."[11]

Historian Ira Berlin noted the importance of what he termed the "re-Africanization" of slaves on tobacco plantations of the Chesapeake region. Protestant missionaries and others visiting the plantations were appalled to observe filed teeth, plaited hair, ritual markings and African music among the slaves, who also spoke a "language peculiar to themselves." In short, as Berlin observes, "Africa had come to the Chesapeake."[12] This return to African rituals and religious beliefs likely gave slaves a way to reconnect to their past and redefine themselves in their own terms, as a way to counter owners' efforts to diminish slaves' self-respect and erase their identity. Ancient African practices such as *vodou*, in particular, would enable slaves to pray to their ancestors, communicate with separated family members, and even take some pleasure in placing curses on those who oppressed them.

By the time the Civil War broke out in 1861, Victor Chambers's mother would have been about forty years old, and perhaps one of the oldest female slaves on the plantation. There were many ways that she and other slaves could have learned of the approaching war. There was a whole communication system referred to by Booker T. Washington as the "grapevine telegraph," which enabled slaves to learn of the impending conflict, often well before their masters. For example, news came from the slave whose duty it was to make regular trips to the post office for mail. Here, he would linger long enough to get the drift of conversations as white people gathered to discuss the news. On the plantation owned by Beverly Barksdale, there would have been many ways through which this "grapevine telegraph" could operate, including the family-owned post office, the Barksdale railroad depot completed in the 1850s, the tobacco plant, and the Brooklyn store where people from throughout the region would come to buy high-quality fabrics and dry goods.

As the war progressed, southern men left to join the ranks of the Confederate army. Colonel Beverly Barksdale, who would have been fifty-three years old in 1861, was one of the ruling elders of Halifax County and considered too old to join the Confederate army. He had written his will in 1860, in the expectation that he would not live much beyond his fifties, and he did in fact not live to see his sixtieth year. His cousin William Barksdale, who was forty years old and also considered an older man for that time, gave up his seat in the U.S. Congress when Mississippi seceded on January 12, 1861. A representative of the state known as a "fortress" of states' rights, and an outspoken advocate of slavery, William Barksdale, who had earlier distinguished himself in military service during the Mexican War, believed it was his duty to join the Confederate army. During his tenure in Congress, he had often engaged in the passionate defense of slavery, noting that black people represented an "inferior race" whose mission was to perform the menial tasks assigned them by their white masters. In one speech he said, "Slavery, in some form, has existed in all ages of the world, and it is sanctioned by Divine authority. We believe it to be right. It is interwoven with our whole social organization, with our very existence as a people; and we are determined, at all hazards, to maintain it."[13]

That belief inspired his fiery defense of slavery as he fought valiantly to defend the Confederacy. After leaving Washington he returned briefly to Mississippi, and he joined the Army of Northern Virginia as a colonel in the Thirteenth Mississippi regiment. He commanded his brigade in all the important battles in Virginia, except for Second Manassas, when he was stationed at Harper's Ferry. In 1862 he was made a brigadier general. While with the Confederate army in Virginia in the autumn and winter of 1862, he may have found time to visit the many Barksdales in that state. Whether William Barksdale saw or had any contact with Victor's mother during the autumn of 1862 will never be known, but their lives would be forever changed several months later, when fate would place them both in the small Pennsylvania town of Gettysburg.

Slaves who watched and listened as the war drew on continued to wear their masks of indifference, but, as Booker T. Washington noted, slaves "gradually threw off the mask." There was "more singing in the slave quarters, and it was bolder, with more ring. . . . They were not afraid to let it be known that the 'freedom' in their songs meant freedom of the body in this world."[14]

As she saw more slaves decide to leave, as conditions on the plantation worsened, as wounded and war-weary Confederate soldiers returned to their homes, and as she learned more about people and networks that could help her regain her freedom, Victor's mother had reason to hope. The defining moment came in the fall of 1862 when she became pregnant, perhaps at a time when she thought her child-bearing days were ended. The fact that this would likely be her last child, and that she might be able to gain not only her own freedom but also that of her child, must have motivated her decision to flee, as well as its timing. It would be far easier to escape while pregnant than to face the dangers and difficulty of trying to evade capture while caring for an infant. This was to be her greatest life-affirming moment, and she was ready.

"Cheer on the weary traveler"

7

We have come over a way that with tears has been watered; . . . out from the gloomy past, till now we stand at last where the white gleam of our bright star is cast.
—*James Weldon Johnson, "Lift Every Voice"*

On January 1, 1863, Victor Chambers's grandmother marked her seventy-sixth birthday. Her parents, who had brought her to the United States from Haiti, were dead, and perhaps her husband had died by then as well. She had at least one other child, Henrietta, who was born shortly after the abduction of her older daughter. Victor's grandmother, whose seventeenth birthday had coincided with the liberation of Haiti, now celebrated her birthday on another auspicious date: the day on which President Abraham Lincoln issued his final Emancipation Proclamation. Unfortunately, as in the case of his first such proclamation issued in 1862, this later version did not apply to border states and could not be enforced in regions held by the Confederacy. It would therefore not have any effect on whether her long-lost daughter would regain her freedom.

Before 1863 was over, the long and eventful life of Victor Chambers's grandmother would be marked by an amazing and dramatic occurrence: the return of her daughter lost to slavery, and the discovery of a new grandson named Victor, born not into slavery but on the battlefield of Gettysburg. The family reunion was brought about not by any governmental law or proclamation, but by the courage, strength, and determination of one woman, whose weary feet would carry her back to the free state of Pennsylvania where her mother and grandparents had arrived seventy years before. Hers would be an arduous journey where fear of capture would hound her every step. Guided by the gleam of the North Star, she traveled by night, probably mourning for other children she would never know, but heartened by the new life of the child she was carrying to freedom.

By the time Victor's mother was preparing her escape, increasing numbers of slaves in Virginia were running away to the North—either alone or with the help of black and white abolitionists, or under the protection of Union forces. Many Virginia slaves joined northern units as they moved through the state. Here they served in a variety of capacities: building and repairing roads and bridges; cooking, sewing, and cleaning for the troops; driving ambulances and carts; and scouting and serving as spies—as did Harriet Tubman (born Araminta Ross), who also served as a cook for the troops and the black laborers supporting those units. In one county of northeastern Virginia, where the proximity of Federal troops was too tempting, almost half of the able-bodied male slaves fled to Union camps between 1861 and 1863.[1]

At the same time, fugitive slaves had to be wary of Union army units, especially as the number of runaways increased and soldiers' supplies dwindled. There were many well-founded stories concerning Union soldiers abusing or even selling runaways back to southern slave catchers.[2]

Once Victor Chambers's mother left the Barksdale plantation, her departure must have caused great consternation to her owners, for she was probably a valued slave, having served the Barksdale family for so many years. Like other plantation owners at that time, the Barksdales worried about possible defections by their slaves and probably took measures to keep them from escaping or running away with Union army units. I saw evidence of the Barksdales' concerns when I visited the restored home of Beverly Barksdale, known as Brooklyn. In the living room is a trap door that is usually covered with a rug. The current owners said that when wounded Union soldiers were brought to the plantation during the later stages of the war, the

Barksdale family kept a rug over the trap door, since that led to the cellar where they kept their slaves hidden, under orders not to make any noise until the northerners were treated and had moved on.

Some plantation owners chained valuable slaves during the night to prevent them from running away. One former slave said that, during the evening hours, his master "sat in his big chair on the porch with a jug of whisky by his side—watching the [slave] quarters to see that none of his slaves started slipping away."[3] Some owners were thoroughly unprepared for what was happening, believing their slaves too docile to flee. One such owner, perplexed by the disappearance of a slave woman whom he had always considered a faithful house servant, could only conclude that "she must have been enticed off by some white men."[4] He had no idea how important freedom was to those who had been denied it for so long.

The deep longing for freedom was eloquently expressed by many of the slaves who managed to escape. Former slave Ambrose Headen said, "During all my slave life I never lost sight of freedom. It was always on my heart; it came to me like a solemn thought, . . . often circumstances . . . stimulated the desire to be free and raised expectations of it."[5] Another runaway, James L. Bradley, explained, "From the time I was 14 years old, I used to think . . . about freedom. It was my heart's desire; I could not keep it out of my mind. Many a sleepless night I have spent in tears, because I was a slave. . . . My heart ached to feel within me the life of liberty."[6] The formidable Harriet Tubman (who, coincidentally, was born in the same general area at about the same date as Victor's mother) proclaimed, "There's two things I got a right to, and these are Death and Liberty. One or the other I mean to have. No one will take me alive [and] I shall fight for my liberty."[7]

Their abiding desire for freedom motivated slaves to flee, but, unfortunately, many failed in their attempts. Those who succeeded were among the most resourceful, gifted, and brave, or merely those able to imagine a future. The word "future" even took on the same aspect of the sacred and the wonderful as did the word "freedom." When Frederick Douglass first dared to think of life beyond the restraints of bondage, he said that "the thought of only being a creature of the present and the past troubled me, and I longed to have a future." To be closed off forever within the confines of the past and the present "is abhorrent to the human mind; it is to the soul . . . what the prison is to the body."[8]

To succeed in the quest for a future and for freedom required great physical stamina, ingenuity, and self-reliance. As a woman over forty, Victor Chambers's mother probably knew that her chances of success were not good. William Still noted that "females undertook three times the risk of failure that males are liable to."[9] Despite the odds, Victor's mother was prepared: she had the will, the skills, and the determination to meet her goal.

The severe punishment for failed fugitives did not abate as the years drew on, despite the war's adverse effect on morale and the economy in the South. In Virginia, in particular, the road to freedom was fraught with danger: armed patrols on horseback, bloodhounds hot on the scent of runaways, and signs at crossroads and on taverns advertising handsome rewards for the capture of runaways. One man, who escaped from a Virginia plantation in May 1863 (about the same time that Victor's mother probably began her journey), was pursued by men with bloodhounds and ultimately caught. The men set the dogs on him and let them bite their victim before taking him to a blacksmith to have an iron ring placed around his ankle. The blacksmith fitted it while the iron was red hot, to make sure it fit well. They also placed a chain with a fifty-pound weight around the man's waist. When he returned to the plantation, the slave was flogged severely every day for a month.[10]

A successful escape had to be carefully planned. Frederick Douglass said that it took him several weeks to prepare his escape from a plantation in Delaware. He made sure not to appear insolent or sulky in front of the master, nor to reveal his sense of anticipation, for fear of making the master suspicious. Douglass had helped other slaves plan their escapes long before he devised his own plan, and he was aware of the active network of people helping slaves move along well-established routes of what became known as the Underground Railroad. Prior to his own escape in 1838, he endured long weeks of tension as he weighed all the risks involved, ensured that all necessary forged papers and disguises were ready, saw that potential logistical

Frederick Douglass

problems were skillfully addressed in advance, and obtained names of free blacks and others who would help him on his way.[11]

Victor's mother probably had the time to plan her own route and method of departure. She was likely headed north into Maryland and onward to Gettysburg, which was long known as a welcoming refuge for runaway slaves. That route would also take her westward from Gettysburg to Chambersburg rather than eastward on a more direct line to Philadelphia. The latter choice would be more dangerous, whereas at Chambersburg there were well-established Underground Railroad networks that could more safely send slaves by train onward to the capital of Harrisburg and ultimately to Philadelphia. Because this was a well-traveled route for those moving along the Underground Railroad, it is likely that she had made advance arrangements with agents of that clandestine operation who were constantly moving through the South at great peril to their own lives.

To maintain the success of the operation, the network used secret codes. Most terms were taken from railroad jargon: "passengers" were helped by "conductors" who led them to "stations" or larger "depots" where they would receive food, shelter, instructions, and perhaps money for moving on to the next stop. There were secret handshakes, passwords, and signals, which changed regularly to avoid possible compromise. Stations were usually located ten to thirty miles apart, or the distance a healthy man could cover in one night. Passengers looked for signals to identify stations: a bright candle in a particular window, or a lighted lantern in a front yard. Agents who ran stations or major depots left few if any written records; they usually hid or destroyed their journals to protect themselves as well as the runaways they harbored.

Throughout the loosely knit network, extremely tight security measures were necessary because spies of both races were everywhere, eager to turn in runaway slaves or expose the secret nature of the operation for money or fame. Sometimes, fugitive slaves would be contacted by Union army intelligence agents during their nocturnal march northward. The value of intelligence provided by runaways was first exploited by Allan Pinkerton, himself a former Underground Railroad agent, who served as the principal intelligence advisor to Major General George B. McClellan during the latter's tenure as commander of the Army of the Potomac. Pinkerton knew that escaped slaves were more than willing to cooperate and often had the most timely information concerning Confederate army deployments, supply points, and defenses. Pinkerton instructed his agents to pay special attention to slaves who were educated and skillful in observing and remembering military details.[12]

Prior to her escape, Victor's mother may have been aware of abolitionist tracts such as the *Liberator* and Frederick Douglass's *North Star*, which were regularly smuggled into the South, and which would have enlightened her about the types of support she could count on along her journey into free territory. It was usually during secret gatherings or prayer meetings that slaves made it known that they were preparing to leave; they did so by singing certain hymns, such as "Steal Away," "Swing Low, Sweet Chariot," and, of course, "Follow the Drinking Gourd"—the Drinking Gourd was a slave name for the constellation of the Big Dipper and the North Star.

Because slaves traveled only at night and because many did not encounter anyone connected with the Underground Railroad until after they crossed the Mason-Dixon line, the North Star was their only guide. On cloudy or rainy nights, they found their way by feeling the moss on trees, knowing that moss grows on the north side of the tree.

Victor's description of his mother's escape is brief: "My mother ran away from the Barksdale plantation and started for the north. She arrived at the town of Gettysburg Adams County Pa on the evening of Tuesday June 30th 1863." There are no further details as to when she left, what routes she followed, whether she was assisted by Underground Railroad agents, or whether she met up with Federal troops along the way. Her decision to leave prior to her baby's birth was a wise one. Many escapes failed because of the presence of babies and small children. Harriet Tubman, who led many slaves out of bondage, always carried a tincture of opium to quiet crying babies, as well as wounded or frightened fugitives.

Among the greatest dangers along Virginia roads were the night riders and bloodhounds. Mounted slave patrols moved throughout the state at night, when they knew slaves would be on the move. They would run down fugitives with their horses, shoot them or tie them to the horses, and drag them, if they survived, to the nearest jail. Some slaves were savagely torn apart by what were often called "Spanish bloodhounds." Slave owners prided themselves in their choice of dogs. One man paid $1,540 for a pack of ten, and another paid $301 for one particularly vicious dog. The dogs were actually a mix of bloodhound and foxhound, and they were ferocious, gaunt and savage-looking animals. Alexander Ross, a naturalist from the North, described these dogs as "larger and more compact than ordinary hounds, with hair straight and sleek as that of the finest race horse, colored between yellow and brown, short-eared, rather long-nosed and built for scenting, quick action and speed." Their owners fed them exclusively on Indian cornmeal to keep them hungry and eager for their next meal.[13]

Slaves used various ways to throw dogs off their scent, including sprinkling hot red pepper powder over their trail. One man carried a special liquid (probably including hot peppers, or the urine of animals feared by the hounds) to prevent the dogs from scenting him. He rubbed it on his legs and feet; when the hounds came near him, they howled and turned back immediately. Because of the hounds' ability to locate and track down their prey, many fugitives walked whenever possible in streams and rivers (hence, the real meaning behind the spiritual "Wade in the Water, Children"). Walking at night, along solitary roads, swamps, and streams, ever fearful of the night riders, hounds, and those eager to turn in runaway slaves for reward money, fugitive slaves spent agonizing hours and days in constant fear for their lives. The testimony of slaves who escaped from the South gives some insight into what Victor Chambers's mother might have experienced. One woman endured a long journey of several months (from Mississippi to Illinois), traveling by night and hiding in thickets during the day. She stopped occasionally at slave huts to beg for food or shelter for a night. She survived mainly on green corn and wild fruit and evaded dogs by wading in ponds and streams. When the water was too deep for wading, she made rafts of logs tied with grapevines or hickory withes, and paddled along. Once in Illinois, where she made her first contact with the Underground Railroad, she rose up and jumped up and down for half an hour, so great was her joy.[14]

The locations of Underground Railroad stations in Virginia where Victor's mother might have stopped during her journey northward remain unknown. Because Virginia was such hostile territory, those who did escape never mentioned specific Underground Railroad stops in that state. Their secrecy endured over the years, so great was their fear of putting other fugitives, as well as conductors and agents, in danger.

Victor's mother may have set out in May, when she was seven months pregnant and there was a greater likelihood that her baby would survive. In clear weather, the moon and starlit sky would have enabled her to follow the westward outline of the Blue Ridge Mountains, as well as the North Star, for direction. During the day, she would probably rest in the woods where she could find shelter from the hot sun and respite from the strain caused by trekking over the steep, undulating hills. Her nocturnal route would take her beneath a variety of trees whose shady canopy would cover her during the day; these included cedar, sycamore, chestnut, oak, tulip poplar, cottonwood, and sweet gum. She may have tried to cover more ground during those days when she found herself in extensive groves of pawpaw trees, which provide a dense, dark shade. When walking beneath the white pines, her feet might have found comfort in their soft carpet of needles. Most often, however, she would likely keep to the rivers, streams, and creeks (known as runs)—not only to evade the hounds but also to avoid the scraggly, twisted branches of mountain laurel and rhododendrons that grew and still grow along their banks.

During her brief moments of respite, she would remain alert to the sounds of horses and hounds, or perhaps soldiers setting up camp. In Virginia at that time, Confederate as well as Union troops would be heading toward their fateful confrontation at Gettysburg. "Young Massa Will" Barksdale and his brigade were out there somewhere as well. Had he seen her and realized she had escaped from his uncle's plantation, he surely would have sent her back to his uncle, and to swift and harsh punishment.

During her trek northward, she would have to be careful of the various streams that could at times be reduced to a narrow trickle but, after heavy rains, develop into wild, surging rivers overflowing their banks. (She would later witness the damage such rains would cause to wounded soldiers lying near the streams at Gettysburg.) She would also be wary of the many wild whitewater rapids from Virginia's rivers draining away from the eastern edge of the Blue Ridge.

Along the way, she could easily have brushed against poison ivy or torn her skin on the underbrush. She may not have found any real shelter for much of the journey, except for the thick underbrush, an isolated hollowed-out tree, or a cave. The bundle she carried over her shoulder would contain cornmeal and perhaps some salt pork, for making mush. She may have been able to catch a few fish and cook them over fires she would always be ready to extinguish and cover up hastily. In addition to green apples and green corn, there were many edible plants and fruits along her path, including huckleberries, bearberries, elderberries, and the ubiquitous daylilies, all portions of which (flower, stalk, and tuber) are edible. She may also have found raspberries but knew not to eat too many of the acid fruit on an empty stomach.

The plantation midwives especially recommended raspberry for pregnant mothers; it reportedly strengthened the uterine wall, prevented nausea, relieved childbirth pain, and enriched the mother's milk. To heal wounds, she could have used yarrow (*Achillea*), which grew throughout the area. While on the plantation, she may have learned how to prepare tinctures from plants known to have healing powers, and included these in her bundle. Two such mixtures used in those days that would have been useful to her were wild indigo (*Baptisia*), as an antiseptic for wounds or fever, and goldenseal (*Hydrastis*), for use as a general tonic and to heal deep wounds and ulcerations. She may also have carried the fresh root of devil's bit (*Helonias*), which pregnant women used to control nausea, stop vomiting, and prevent miscarriages. That plant would have been available in the Virginia woods at that time of year and familiar to the midwives.[15]

While Victor Chambers's mother was on her northerly path, the Confederate and Union armies were following almost parallel routes from Virginia into Maryland and, ultimately, to Pennsylvania. The southerners were savoring their recent victory at Chancellorsville, where their triumphal army, under superior leadership, had defeated and demoralized the larger northern units, just as they had done in December 1862 at Fredericksburg.

By early June, General William Barksdale was leading his men westward from the vicinity of Chancellorsville toward the Blue Ridge. Other Confederate troops were moving toward Culpeper, their spirits high as they entered Brandy Station, where they staged a parade and mock battle for the admiring crowds. The men were all in their finest attire, with plumes and flags dancing in the air, while the ladies greeted them from their porches and verandas. Children showered flowers on their path, and there were cheers everywhere. This magnificent spectacle was followed that evening by a ball held in the open air, where the soldiers and ladies danced by the light of wood fires.[16]

While their Confederate counterparts were enjoying the festive evening and the lovely surroundings, two Union army cavalry divisions moved toward the Confederate camp at Brandy Station and took General J. E. B. Stuart and his men completely by surprise. The Richmond *Examiner* admitted that this Union assault narrowly missed being a great disaster. It was a victory that the northerners needed, since it afforded their cavalry a chance to prove its worth and enabled them to regain confidence in themselves and their commanders.

During that engagement, the Union army obtained valuable intelligence that ultimately led to their encounter with the Confederates at Gettysburg. According to Edward Coddington, the information came from "a Negro servant, captured from an officer in Stuart's artillery"; this man furnished "remarkably reliable intelligence" about Confederate army locations and strength. Other sources identify this man as Charlie Wright. Mr. Wright noted specifically that "Ewell's Corps has passed Brandy Station the day before the fight and that Longstreet was now coming up."[17] He also identified more than a dozen Confederate regiments from these two units. While he did not have access to key strategic intelligence relating to General Lee's ultimate plans and intentions, Mr. Wright did provide much-needed tactical indications that two major elements of the Confederate army had moved from Culpeper en route to Maryland. (Many former Union army officers, as well as historians, have since either ignored or downplayed Mr. Wright's role in the Union decision to move northward in pursuit of Lee. Although Coddington failed to identify the "Negro servant" by name, he nonetheless castigated those officers who later invented all kinds of stories about the source of the information, ranging from documents stolen in General Stuart's desk to an outline found in an old tobacco pouch. Coddington referred to all these "increasingly astonishing" stories as "embellishments," or, worse yet, "double talk."[18] I wonder, if the intelligence had come from a white man, would its source have been more openly acknowledged.

Major General Joseph Hooker, who in January 1863 had replaced General Ambrose Burnside, after the disgraceful northern defeat at Fredericksburg, concluded that General Lee and his troops were moving north into Maryland. Those Union army elements that had stayed behind in the vicinity of Fredericksburg, including my great-grandfather's New York regiment, left abruptly when word came from Washington to move immediately and pursue the southern troops moving toward the Potomac. In the scorching heat, field commanders constantly urged the men to move faster. Many fell from heat stroke while others, with sore and blistered feet, continued the seventeen-hour nonstop march. Despite their fatigue, the soldiers' spirits were high, and many even had the energy to sing as they marched along.[19]

Their morale was once again boosted by the warm reception they received after they crossed the Potomac into Maryland. Their march into Frederick took on a triumphal air. Houses were draped with flags; children and young girls handed flowers to the soldiers; and people sang patriotic songs as bands played. The change in spirit and attitude of the Union troops as they moved steadily northward was similar to the changes that were probably affecting Victor Chambers's mother as she, too, approached the Pennsylvania border. Now, like the northern troops, her march was taking on a jubilant, triumphal air of boundless joy—more attuned to the words and joyful tone of the spiritual,

> Let us cheer on the weary traveler!
> Let us cheer on the weary traveler,
> Along the heavenly way!

The joy of Victor's mother's must have been boundless; she was returning to the land of her lost childhood, and was about to give birth to a child who would be free and able to pursue his or her own destiny. Her happiness in finally crossing into free territory must have been similar to that of Harriet Tubman, who, upon crossing into Pennsylvania early in the morning, exclaimed, "I looked at my hands to see if I was the same person! There was such a glory over everything. The sun came up like gold through the trees, and I felt like I was in Heaven!"[20]

"We can never forget what they did here"

8

> The world . . . can never forget what they did here. It is for us the living . . . to be dedicated to the . . . great task remaining before us. We here resolve that these dead shall not have died in vain . . . that this nation, under God, shall have a new birth of freedom.
> —*Abraham Lincoln, Gettysburg Address*

The route being followed by Victor Chambers's mother would lead her to a region of Pennsylvania that had long been a haven for those seeking refuge from slavery, and a strategic stop for those moving north or west along the Underground Railroad. Victor Chambers wrote:

> My mother . . . arrived at the town of Gettysburg Adams County Pa on the evening of Tuesday June 30th 1863.

Located between the Catoctin Mountains to the east and the South Mountain link of the Appalachians to the west, Gettysburg lies in a gently sloping valley that serves as a natural focal point for roads leading north, south, east, and west. The residence built in 1774 by Presbyterian minister Alexander Dobbin had been home to the first black slaves in the region and was later used by Dobbin's descendants as an Underground Railroad depot. Along a stairway of the Dobbin house, which is now a restaurant, are sliding wall shelves behind which runaway slaves could find protection.[1] If, as is most probable, Victor's mother approached the town from the south, along its main road, she may have stopped at the Dobbin House to rest and receive instructions before continuing toward the western part of town, where most of the town's black residents were concentrated.

While the Dobbin house was a smaller "depot," there was a larger Underground Railroad "station" at Gettysburg as well; namely, the McAllister mill. A memoir by Theodore McAllister in 1912 indicated that his family's mill had been used since at least 1850 as a major stopping-off site for slaves on their way north. The large building contained food, clothing, and other provisions for runaways and offered them a place to rest as well.[2]

As a result of the continual movement of slaves through the town, as well as the economic opportunities there, the black population of Gettysburg had surged dramatically between the early 1800s and the Civil War. While there were only eight "colored" taxpayers there listed in the Adams County tax books between 1806 and 1815, census figures for 1840 showed 21 black heads of household and 162 other free blacks living in Gettysburg. By 1860, there were 35 black children attending schools in Gettysburg; about the same number had to work to support their families. That year's census listed 186 black people as residents, 68 of whom were identified as employed. These included people identified as day laborers, domestic servants, servants, hostlers, cooks, waiters, and one each in the categories of nurse, clergyman, bricklayer, confectioner, janitor, shoemaker, teamster, and wagon maker. Twenty black families owned real estate; most of them lived in the western part of town,[3] which today remains largely populated by African-Americans.

Some of the farms on Cemetery Ridge close to the Chambersburg Pike, which saw the first skirmishes of the battle, were owned by black families. At least two of these families were active in the Underground Railroad. St. Paul's A.M.E. Church in this same area was a major station for slaves en route to freedom.

One of the homes in this western part of town was owned by a young man named Alfred Palm. His wife (referred to in census records as his "common-law" wife, as was the practice of many white census takers in those days) was named Margaret Divit. Their son was three years old when the Confederates marched into town on July 1, 1863. Because Margaret Divit Palm wore the sky blue coat of an officer of the War of 1812 during her Underground Railroad operations, she became known as "Maggie Bluecoat." She carried a rifle and courageously fought off slave owners and kidnappers who tried many times to abduct her and carry her off into slavery. She often carried out her Underground Railroad activities in concert with the Dobbin family. According to black residents whom I interviewed at St. Paul's A.M.E. church, Maggie Palm sometimes worked as a maid for the head of the nearby Lutheran Seminary, who reportedly kept her hidden safely at the seminary for the duration of the battle.[4]

Another important black resident of this part of town was a man named Basil Biggs, who had been born in Baltimore but moved to Gettysburg in 1856 so that his children could be educated. A tenant farmer on the McPherson property, Mr. Biggs used his barn to hide runaway slaves during the day. At night, he would take them to the next Underground Railroad stop en route to Canada, or to safe train passage in Chambersburg, west of Gettysburg.[5]

During the latter half of June, as southern forces were moving into Pennsylvania, the booming of cannon fire could be heard with increasing frequency, and there were rumors everywhere of approaching rebel forces. Victor Chambers's mother no doubt heard the cannon fire, and perhaps the rumors as well. Despite all this, she had nowhere to go but straight ahead. On June 18, Dr. Philip Schaff, a white minister in nearby Mercersburg (often referred to as "Little Africa" because of the large number of people of African descent living there at the time), wrote in his diary, "Now the whole veteran army of Lee is said to be crossing the Potomac and crossing into Pennsylvania. We are cut off from all mail communication and dependent on rumors. The poor Negroes, the innocent cause of the war, are trembling like leaves and flying with their little bundles to the mountains, especially the runaways from Virginia, from fear of being captured as contraband and sold in the south." On the next day, Schaff wrote that homes and public places had been ransacked by the approaching southern troops; that cattle and provisions had been "stolen without mercy"; and that "Negroes (were) captured and carried back into slavery—even those born and raised on free soil."[6]

"Thousands" of free blacks fled the Cumberland Valley and headed north to the capital of Harrisburg, seeking refuge from troops they knew would seize them and sell them as slaves. The official record of the war notes that, before Confederate troops began their march toward Gettysburg, General James Longstreet ordered General George Pickett to "bring along the contraband."[7]

While the Confederates were scouring fields and small towns for black residents, one group of southern soldiers was thwarted in its efforts, thanks to the courage of a group of black women as well as the white townspeople of Greencastle, located between Chambersburg and Gettysburg. A Confederate chaplain and four soldiers drove into that town with a wagon filled with between thirty and forty black women and children whom they had captured at Chambersburg. When the townspeople of Greencastle saw what was happening, they surprised and disarmed the soldiers, locked them in jail, and set the women and children free. When Confederate General Albert Jenkins learned of this, he demanded fifty thousand dollars from the town for his lost contraband and threatened to burn down the town if the money was not provided. Upon hearing of this threat, some of the black women contacted town leaders and, like the noble Burghers of Calais immortalized by the French sculptor Rodin, selflessly offered to give themselves up in order to save the town. The town leaders refused to accept this courageous offer. Fortunately for the town and the women, Jenkins and his men were ordered to move at great haste toward Gettysburg and were never able to exact their vengeance.[8]

By the time the Confederate troops reached Gettysburg, they had taken at least fifty of the town's black residents, who were later sent to southern slave markets. Most other African-Americans had already fled. The great majority of these people never returned to Gettysburg. After the battle, the town's black population dropped from 186 to only 64—something that was not found newsworthy by the local papers. As was the case before the battle, coverage of blacks in the Gettysburg press was limited to racist jokes in the "Humor" section. For example, throughout the month of June 1863, the *Gettysburg Compiler* carried numerous cartoons and jokes about black men volunteering to serve in the military, in response to Governor Curtin's call for new recruits.

Because the town's white residents were used to viewing their black counterparts mainly as objects of mockery, they did not grasp the imminent, dire threat that the southern advance posed to the black population. That is perhaps why the wartime diary of young Tillie Alleman depicted the frenzied departure of black residents as something to laugh at: "It was amusing to behold the conduct of the colored people. . . . They regarded the rebels as having an especial hatred toward them, and they believed that if they fell into their hands, annihilation was sure. . . . I can see them yet; men and women with bundles . . . slung across their backs . . . The greatest consternation was depicted on all their countenances as they hurried along; crowding, and running against each other in their confusion; children stumbling, falling and crying."[9] Another resident, Catherine Mary White Foster, wrote that in their efforts to evade the Confederates, the fleeing black residents appeared to be engaged in some type of game, playing "hiding and peeping all this time." She added, "if time permitted, we might insert some curious scenes which occurred among them."[10]

As Victor Chambers's mother entered the town, most of the town's black residents would have fled north. Those who remained behind were the elderly, the very sick or frail, and those with severe physical disabilities; in short, those who were unable to leave or who did not believe that the southerners would be interested in taking them.[11] In the ninth month of her pregnancy, Victor's mother probably found her condition to be a protection against capture as well.

That night before the battle, the townspeople of Gettysburg were unaware of what the next day would bring. The Reverend Doctor Henry E. Jacobs of Pennsylvania College (now Gettysburg College) took his telescope to Seminary Hill west of town, where he climbed up to the observatory at the Lutheran Theological Seminary. From this vantage point, he could see the campfires of the Confederates to the west.

Somewhere that night, Victor Chambers's mother must have found a place to sleep, perhaps on the newly cut sheaves in the nearby wheat fields, or in the woods. There were some reports of stars falling that night, but not as dramatically as the falling stars that

Victor's mother had seen in November 1833—her sixth year as a slave. Had she seen the stars over Gettysburg on the night of June 30, she might have considered that an omen. Several eyewitnesses said that a spirit of unrest seemed to prevail everywhere on the next day. The morning was unusually quiet, and the stillness oppressive. Dr. Jacobs noted that clouds filled the sky, and that there was a very gentle breeze from the south.[12]

Prior to the Confederate march down the Chambersburg Pike, a portion of the Union troops, led by General John Buford's cavalry division, had moved toward Gettysburg from the south, while other Union troops were approaching from the southeast. During these early morning hours, Victor's mother was attempting to leave Gettysburg and move toward the Chambersburg Pike, but she was stopped by Buford's men.

> On Wednesday morning, July first, she started to leave the place, but was overtaken by the advance of Buford's cavalry just westward of Gettysburg on the Chambersburg Town Pike. She could go no farther.
>
> Mother has told me that from where she stood she could see the advancing regiments of A. P. Hill's Corps of 35,000 men, approaching from the North West.

As Confederate units approached from the west, people in the town could hear sounds of cannon fire and bursts of artillery fire. The streets of Gettysburg were filled with frightened people, hearing the dreadful sounds of battle nearby, yet scarcely realizing the enormity of the battle soon to be fought at their doorsteps. As more people panicked and ran about shouting and screaming, Buford's men told them to stay off the streets and not leave town. Young Billy Bayly and his friends, perched on a fence near a raspberry patch on the Chambersburg Pike, were awe-struck when they saw "masses of [Confederate] troops and clouds of dust; the first wave swelled into successive waves, gray masses with the glint of steel as the sun struck the gun barrels, filling the highway, spreading out into the fields, and still coming on and on, wave after wave, bellow after bellow."[13]

Union General John Fulton Reynolds, who was moving a column

of men from the south in order to assess the situation and confer with Buford, led his men away from the center of town and toward the west, across the fields leading toward the seminary. Reynolds, who was from nearby Lancaster, knew this region well and had spent much of his youth riding and hunting in the countryside and woods of Gettysburg. Revered by his men as one of the few "soldier generals" of the Union army, Reynolds had once been comman-dant of cadets at West Point.

General John F. Reynolds

An aide, Major Joseph C. Rosen-garter, described Reynolds as a "lithe and athletic man," well over six feet tall, who could pick up a glove from the ground at full gallop.[14] Lieutenant Frank A. Haskell described Reynolds as "the very beau ideal of the gallant general. Mounted upon a superb black horse, with his head thrown back and his great black eyes flashing, he was every-where in the field, seeing all things and giving commands in per-son."[15] Union army General Joshua Chamberlain said in 1899 that, at the Battle of Second Bull Run, or Second Manassas, Reynolds had been captured and spent six weeks at the infamous Libby Prison in Richmond. Chamberlain added that Reynolds was subsequently freed in a prisoner exchange for Confederate William Barksdale.[16]

As Reynolds rode toward the eastern edge of McPherson's Woods, his First Corps moved into line, with Reynolds himself deploying the famed Iron Brigade.[17] According to Victor Chambers's letters, his mother was nearby, seeking shelter in the woods.

> She was talking to General John F. Reynolds when he was shot from his horse, just south of the Chambersburg Road. He was telling her to get out from under the trees, for she might be killed. He fell into her arms from his horse. She broke the fall.

Reynolds, who was known for staying near the front line, was hit while astride his horse at the edge of the woods. Steady Confederate fire spread smoke everywhere, making it difficult to see. Just before he was hit, about a thousand rebel troops from Alabama and Tennessee were moving through the woods. Military historian and Gettysburg expert Edwin Coddington and Reynolds biographer Edward R. Nichols have documented the discrepancies in reports by various aides to General Reynolds regarding his death. Some claimed it was caused by a sharpshooter, while others believed it was due to the volley of shots coming from the Confederate troops moving through the woods. Major Rosengarter changed his version of the event twice. Many accounts of the battle of Gettysburg were written by those with scores to settle or those seeking personal gain and perhaps a place in history. As a result, some of their information has since been discounted. Nevertheless, they all help to shed light on a battle whose complete story will perhaps never be known.

Charles Veil, an orderly, wrote to Reynolds's sisters stating that he was the only person present at the time of the general's death. The official war record states, however, that General Abner Doubleday, who assumed command of the First Corps upon Reynolds's death, "arrived on the ground about the time, or very soon after, General Reynolds fell."[18] While perusing newspaper articles at the Adams County Historical Society, I found an obituary of General W. W. Dudley, in the *Gettysburg Compiler* of December 22, 1909; it stated that Dudley's "regiment was among the first troops of the First Corps to arrive on the first day's battle. . . . He saw General Reynolds shot."[19]

While no one can know how many were indeed present, it was Sergeant Veil's story that General Reynolds's surviving sisters believed. Being from a prominent and influential family, the two sisters intervened with President Lincoln and Secretary of War Stanton to have Veil promoted and commissioned as an officer.[20] Veil's memoir, written forty-five years after the battle, elaborates on the circumstances of the general's death: "As he rode into the edge of the woods, ... he turned in his saddle, looking toward the rear . . . when he was struck by a minie ball and fell from his horse." Veil added, "This is an authentic account . . . and can be verified by no other living person than myself, having been the only person directly present when the general fell."[21]

No accounts other than the Chambers letter mention the presence of a black woman. Timothy Smith, a historian at the Gettysburg National Military Park, said that this does not necessarily mean that Victor Chambers's account is inaccurate. Smith noted that all the early accounts were written by the military, for the military, and about the military; thus, the presence of any civilian would not have been noteworthy. He suggested two hypotheses. One is that Victor Chambers's mother may have been near another officer who was hit and, hearing later about Reynolds's death, assumed it was Reynolds that she had seen. Second, if it were indeed Reynolds who told her to move away from the trees, that conversation would probably have taken place about fifteen minutes before he was hit. Smith explained that, at any time closer to his death, Reynolds would have been too involved in the fighting to notice or speak to anyone.

Other Civil War experts and historians to whom I spoke discounted Victor Chambers's statement about Reynolds falling into his mother's arms, considering it probably an "embellishment," much like the flourishes of his flowing handwriting style. At the same time, the situation described by Victor Chambers cannot completely be dismissed, because no one will ever know what exactly happened at this particular moment of the battle.

General Reynolds was not the first to die in the opening hours of the battle. According to Union Private Augustus Buell's breathtaking account of the action that first morning, the line of northern troops was easily broken by advancing rebel troops. Buell said he could see

> up and down the line, men reeling and falling, splinters flying from wheels and axles where bullets hit; in the rear, horses tearing and plunging, mad with wounds or terror; drivers yelling, shells bursting, shot shrieking overhead; . . . bullets hissing, humming and whistling everywhere; cannon roaring, crash upon crash and peal upon peal; smoke, dust, splinters, blood, wreck and carnage-indescribable . . . an undulating field, almost as far as the eye could reach, with a long, low gray line creeping toward us,

fringed with fire. . . . That same sun, that a day before had been shining to cure the wheat-fields of the harvest of peace, now glared to pierce the gray pall of battle's powder smoke, or to bloat the corpses of the battle's victims.[22]

Numerous accounts refer to the great heat of that day, the smoke and fire from artillery making the air even more oppressive. By nightfall, the battle sounds were at last muted and the heat subsided, the groans of wounded and dying men blending with the sounds of the countryside. During that ghostly night, Victor Chambers's mother probably sought refuge from the day's battle. Like her, other women had been caught up in the fighting and unable to leave the battlefield. Amelia Harmon and her aunt, who lived in the McLean house overlooking Willoughby Run, had let Union troops use their home earlier in the day. Later, Confederate troops took over the house, forcing Amelia and her aunt into the midst of the battle. Surrounded by flying bullets and troops shouting at them to get out of the way or be killed, the two women managed to work their way to the Confederate rear, where they received food and shelter. Amelia wrote, "We were doubtless the only persons on the Union side who were fed from General Lee's commissary during the battle of Gettysburg."[23]

Victor Chambers's mother may have found similar arrangements, perhaps helped by the many black men and women who worked for both armies as cooks, laborers, or wagon drivers. During that first night, she may also have heard wafting through the warm night air the new song composed by General Daniel Butterfield. Referred to by the men as "Butterfield's Lullaby," it was meant to be conducive to sleep and rest. The words to the repeated three-note pattern were: "Go to sleep. Go to sleep." This tune later became known as "Taps," now associated not only with the end of the day, but also with death and military funerals. It may also have been the first lullaby heard by the baby soon to be born on this battlefield where so many would sleep forever.

"My mother could not
get away from the field"

9

The Civil War soldier was a quite ordinary
human being rendered extraordinary by his
confrontation with fate, coming to grips with
something larger than himself. . . . He displayed heroism without indulging in heroics.
—*Bruce Catton, America Goes to War*

The second day of the battle saw serious losses for the Confederate
cause, among them the death of General William Barksdale of
Mississippi and the wounding of General John Bell Hood of Texas.
Victor Chambers learned about these events not only from his moth-
er but also through his friendship with a man who had been at
Gettysburg with General Hood.

In his letters, Victor Chambers explained that a man named
Armstead Lewis, who preceded Victor in his job as janitor at a school
in Providence, "was the body servant of the Rebel General J.B. Hood,
and was with him at Gettysburg." Like others who met Victor
Chambers over the years, Mr. Lewis was obviously impressed by the
younger man's knowledge about Gettysburg, as well as by the unique
story of his birth on the battlefield. Even though he had sons of his
own, Armstead Lewis gave Victor a valuable memento of his service
at Gettysburg. Victor noted, "I have his old Bible here now. He had it
in his pocket on that memorable Thursday afternoon [the second day
of the battle]."

The route that took Mr. Lewis from a Virginia plantation to service
for the Confederacy, and ultimately to Rhode Island, is as fascinating
as the stories of many other African-Americans of that era, who went

to great lengths in search of freedom. Armstead Lewis was born on a plantation owned by Colonel Ned Wallace, on the bank of the Rappahannock River, near Fredericksburg. A domestic slave as a youth, he later became his owner's body servant when the war broke out.[1] Usually only the most affluent had their own body servants, who acted as attendants and bodyguards. Legends abounded regarding these most valuable slaves, known for their bravery in battle and loyalty to their masters. Although they were referred to as "body servants" rather than slaves, the men in that category saw no distinction in the terms. These courageous men sought freedom whenever the opportunity arose, often to the astonishment of their masters, who could not reconcile the fidelity of these men with their overriding desire for freedom.

When Mr. Lewis's owner was either killed or incapacitated, he was sent by Confederate army commanders to a camp where he was made body servant to General John Bell Hood of Texas.[2] His assignment to serve this West Point graduate, who was considered a "rising star" in the Confederacy and protégé of Robert E. Lee when both served in the United States army in Texas,[3] indicates that Mr. Lewis must have been an impressive man. He was with Hood at Gettysburg, but eventually found an opportunity to escape. He joined the Union army, where he served in a transport unit, probably driving or repairing wagons or carts, as did many other black men serving in the Union army. Mr. Lewis settled in Boston after the war; there he learned that a young woman who had been a slave on a plantation near his own had made her way to Providence (as had many other former slaves, hoping for better jobs in the North). Mr. Lewis moved to Rhode Island and married the young woman. It was through political connections that he was "rewarded" with what was considered at that time a plum job for a black man—that of a janitor in the public school system in Providence. When Armstead Lewis died, one Providence newspaper heralded him as a "man who nursed officers in the thick of the Civil War" and referred to him as "one of the oldest and best known colored residents of this city."[4]

In recounting what Armstead Lewis had told him about the second day of the battle, Victor wrote,

> Hood's Texans were cutting you all to pieces at the Trostle
> House, the Peach Orchard, the Wheat Field and Little
> Round Top. Mr. Lewis told me that Gen. Hood swore oaths
> of a terrible hue, when he saw the old Sixth Corps coming
> down the Baltimore Pike under Sedgwick. And it saved the
> day.

Victor's mother had also spoken to her son about Hood's fierce
attack against the Third Corps:

> How fearful must have been the fight when your regiment
> met Hood at Weed's Hill, and Sickles' line was forced back
> to the Wentz house. My mother has shown me where the
> old glorious Third stood. I have heard her say that in the
> yard of a Trostle near Weed's Hill she stood and counted
> 203 dead alone, and that was nothing!

That second day was a hot, tiring, and frustrating day for General
Hood. Before he and his men could move on or rest from one difficult engagement, General Longstreet kept them waiting for new
orders. After hours waiting in the hot sun, Hood received orders to
move toward Gettysburg at right angles along the Emmitsburg
Road—orders that in Hood's view would only lead to unnecessary loss
of lives if his men had to move through the well-protected and fortified Union artillery positions.[5] Because Hood's scouts had told him
earlier in the day that there were no Union soldiers on Little Round
Top, Hood wanted to move his men through open pasture around the
Round Top, to strike at the enemy's flank and rear.[6] But Longstreet
refused to listen to Hood's suggestions, reiterating that the orders had
come directly from Lee: "We must obey the orders of General Lee."[7]
Contrary to Lee's orders, however, Hood and his men eventually
broke away from the Emmitsburg Road and toward Little Round Top
and Devil's Den. As heavy shelling pelted down all around his units,
one shell broke above Hood's head, and the fragments tore into his
arm.[8] As he was carried from the field, his unit seemed to lose its focus
and direction. Hood's pain and frustration may well have caused him
to "utter oaths of a terrible hue," as Armstead Lewis stated.

As for General William Barksdale, Victor simply states that:

> [General] Barksdale . . . commanded a brigade in Longstreet's Corps. And was killed at Gettysburg . . . while leading a charge upon the works of the Second Corps at Gettysburg, July 2nd, 1863—Hancock's Corps.

Victor also interjected the following information, concerning his mother's relationship with Barksdale, the nephew of her owner:

> [She] was well acquainted with young Massa Will Barksdale.

Victor's choice of words is intriguing. Because he was writing to an elderly man whom he had never met, Victor obviously did not want to reveal any intimate secrets about his mother's past as a slave if, indeed, she had shared these in much detail with her son. At the same time, however, it appears that he wanted to make a point with his reader. In the sentence where he links Barksdale and his mother, Victor uses the term "young Massa Will" rather than "General Barksdale," perhaps to reveal that Victor may have been aware of a more intimate and sinister aspect of his mother's relationship with Barksdale.

Those who knew William Barksdale described him as a man of great passion for the southern cause, who could be insulting and demeaning to those who did not share his views, and at the same time loyal and gentle to his friends and family. He was born in Tennessee, where his family had moved after leaving Halifax County, Virginia. After his father's death, the sixteen- year-old William accompanied his two older brothers to Mississippi. After studying law in Columbus, Mississippi, he was admitted to the bar and soon became involved in politics. He also served as editor of the *Columbus Democrat*, which gave him an outlet for voicing his staunch states'-rights and secessionist views. During the Mexican War, he served in the United States army and reached the grade of captain. In 1852 he was a delegate to the Democratic National Convention, and in 1853 he was elected to the United States Senate, where his positions often put him at odds with moderate northern Republicans.[9] In a speech on the Senate floor, he referred to the superior economic and social situation of the South.[10] On at least one occasion, he came to blows with Senate colleagues on the issue of slavery, and he frequently used insulting language in referring to his political foes.

Before his entry into politics, William Barksdale had married Narcissa Saunders of Louisiana. Shortly before his death, he told an attending Union army surgeon: "Tell [my wife] that my last words were of love to her."[11] When news of his death reached the Confederate lines, one of his men described Barksdale as "gentle as a woman and brave as a lion . . . . He never failed to lead his brigade personally in battle. . . . General Barksdale was one of the greatest and bravest of men . . . Oh! How we loved him and mourned his death."[12]

Earlier in the day, Barksdale, like Hood, had become frustrated by his superiors' delay in sending him into action. Several times, he implored General Lafayette McLaws, "General, let me go; General, let me go!" When he finally received orders from Longstreet to go forward, those nearby described Barksdale's face as "radiant with joy."[13] A large, heavyset man, balding with long wisps of white hair blowing about his head, Barksdale addressed his men, telling them that they were about to begin "a heroic undertaking [in which] most of us will bite the dust." He added, "If there is a man here that feels this is too much for him, just step two paces to the front and I will excuse him." None stepped forward.[14]

Barksdale ordered his men to wait for the command "Halt, ready, fire! Then without command, you will charge with the bayonet."[15] This perfectly executed charge was described by one colleague as "the most magnificent charge of the war." Another Confederate officer said, "I never saw anything equal the dash and heroism of the Mississippians. [Barksdale] was in front of his brigade, hat off, his long white hair" wafting like a plume in the wind. After breaking though line after line of Union defenses and smashing Union positions at the Peach Orchard, Barksdale exhorted his men not to lose heart: "Brave Mississippians, one more charge and the day is ours!"[16] Suddenly, however, he was struck by fire from a New York unit under the Second Corps led by General Winfield Scott Hancock.

As General Barksdale's strength ebbed away, so did the momentum of his troops.

At a Gettysburg reunion many years after the war, a Union army colonel said that Barksdale's was "the grandest charge that was ever seen by mortal man . . . Nothing we could do seemed to confuse or halt Barksdale's veterans. Nothing daunted Barksdale and his men . . . I would like to shake the hand of every member of the Barksdale brigade who is here today . . . they are the bravest men I ever met or ever expect to meet."[17]

To a northern soldier who found Barksdale lying wounded on the battlefield and who offered him some water, the general whispered, "How kind you are, how kind you are!" Another Union soldier commented, "One need not fight any the less stoughtly because of being a gentleman."[18] A Harrisburg newspaper, commenting on Barksdale's death, noted the general's reputation for being "an uncompromising champion of the most advanced school of Southern rights—a genuine fire-eater . . . but, withal, a suave and courteous gentleman of unsullied honor and undoubted bravery."[19]

Barksdale had been carried by stretcher to a house in the rear of the Federal lines. Because the house was full, he had to be placed on the

Confederate veterans "re-enacting" a charge at the reunion
50 years after the Battle of Gettysburg

ground near the house. Northern doctors checked on him regularly throughout the night. He died at a time when the doctors were busy elsewhere. On the night of General Barksdale's death, the field was covered in all manner of filth and body parts of men, horses, and mules. While hogs tore at the dead bodies, looters roamed the field seeking out souvenirs. By morning, the gold braid, buttons, and shirt studs with Masonic emblems had disappeared from General Barksdale's uniform.[20]

That night, Victor's mother may have heard soldiers' conversations regarding Barksdale's demise. She no doubt was fearful, with no one but God to console her as she tried to find some rest from the horror of the battlefield. Like the men around her, she may have found solace in the sweet tenor voice of a Confederate soldier who sang hymns to comfort his wounded comrades. As he closed his recital with the song "When This Cruel War is Over," men on both sides cheered and applauded.[21]

As he walked over the field in the early morning hours of the third and last day of the battle, Lieutenant George Benedict of Vermont, who had served in Congress with William Barksdale, recognized the General's "bald head and broad face, with open unblinking eyes. . . . There he lay alone, without a comrade to brush the flies from his corpse."[22]

10

"This nation shall have a new birth of freedom"

[A]mong strangers, uncared for, unknown.
Even the birds that used to sweetly sing
Are silent . . .
No one but Mother can cheer me today. . . .
Mother would console me, if she were here.
—"Mother Would Console Me," Civil War song

Victor Chambers noted that his mother remained on the battle-field throughout the three-day ordeal:

My mother could not get away from the field.

The third day of the battle was particularly horrific for those on or near the scene of carnage and desolation. The heat intensified as the day progressed, and bodies of dead and decaying men and animals covered the ground. Gravediggers rushed about, dragging bodies into long, shallow trenches. The carcasses of horses and mules were burned in large heaps, the smoke from these fires adding to the putrid stench that permeated the atmosphere.

Later in the day, during the two-hour artillery attack in which a powerful line of Confederate cannons and howitzers fired against Union positions[1] in preparation for the ill-fated march now known as Pickett's charge, townspeople hid in their cellars in an effort to drown out the thundering cannons, fearful that the heavens and earth were crashing together. In his memoir, Confederate Colonel William C. Oates wrote that, throughout the cannonade attack, "the ground fairly trembled, the air was sulphurous and full of smoke . . . for two hours the earth was torn in holes by the bursting shells."[2] After the Union army repulsed the valiant but tragic advance of Confederates across the open fields, soldiers on both sides gradually became aware of the fact that there would be no more fighting. The battle was over. Cheers broke out as the news spread, and men on the Union side spontaneously began to sing "John Brown's Body," with the words "Glory, glory, hallelujah!" resounding over the battle-scarred terrain.[3] Later that night, those present on the battlefield were struck by the silence, broken only by the screams and moans of the wounded and dying. At one point, a military band played the gentle tune of "Home, Sweet Home," which must have sounded especially sweet to Victor's mother.[4]

Victor Chambers's mother had to endure days that in many ways were more frightful than the three days of combat. She wandered over the scene of the battle to see if there were some way she could help those in distress.

> Wounded soldiers were lying where they had fallen 2 days previous, crying for water and slowly bleeding to death. And the temperature all 3 days stood 95 in the shade.
>
> Mother says dead men were piled up in heaps like bound sheaves of wheat in the harvest field.
>
> After the 3 days fight was over, she wandered over the bloody field everywhere looking at the dead and wounded. I have heard her say many a time it was hell, hell. Once seen, <u>never</u> forgotten. Dead men, dead horses, wounded and dying men wherever she went. She was giving a poor soldier a drink, and he died with the first swallow.

After the battle, there were more than thirty thousand wounded and ten thousand missing or captured. About seven thousand men died on the battlefield, while approximately another three thousand died later of their wounds. More than three thousand horses and animals were dead. Some of the dead men and animals remained

Bodies of soldiers killed in battle at Gettysburg await burial

unburied until July 7.[5] The number of wounded exceeded the population not just of Gettysburg, but of all of Adams County.

Surgeons, wounded soldiers, and local residents surveyed the situation before them and found it overwhelming. Young Tillie Pierce said she awoke on July 4 to find herself "in a strange and blighted land."[6] A Union army medical officer wrote in a dispatch to Washington that the ten days after the battle were witness to "the

Dead horses near the scene of Pickett's Charge

greatest amount of human suffering known to this nation since its birth."[7]

At about noon on Saturday, July 4, and well into the next day, the area was hit with torrential storms accompanied by thunder as loud as the cannon fire heard during the battle. Flash floods helped to wash away some of the blood from fields but unfortunately also drowned men who had managed to move next to small streams for comfort. After the rains subsided, groans and cries from injured Confederate soldiers could be heard coming from the field over which Pickett's charge had been made. Wounded Union soldiers were scattered all over the muddy field, with no water, no food, no blankets or tents to ease their discomfort. Those in need of amputations of arms or legs were moved to primitive field hospitals where exhausted surgeons were busy sawing off limbs as fast as possible. Soldiers with serious head wounds were set aside to die, since there was no way to treat that type of injury.[8]

Makeshift hospitals were set up all over town. Every church, public or commercial building, school, farm, and private home had been taken over for the care of the wounded. Town residents blocked their ears to muffle the anguished cries emanating from these places. Journalists and others who observed the town after the battle spoke of the toll it took on the people of the town, many of whom walked around as if in a dream, with stunned looks on their faces. For soldiers remaining on the field, help was slow in coming. Many local farmers, angry at both sides for destroying their land and barns, agreed to provide bread to the soldiers, but only for exorbitant prices.

Women from Gettysburg and elsewhere began arriving on the scene to provide solace for the wounded. Even though she had a large family of her own to feed, Fanny Buehler set up a large table in front of her house and covered it with food, free of charge for anyone who passed by. She regularly replenished the tea, coffee, soup, oatmeal, and cornmeal gruel, as needed.[9]

Fourteen nuns from a nursing order known as the Sisters of Charity arrived from nearby Emmitsburg shortly after the end of the fighting, bearing much-needed medical supplies, proving to be of enormous help to the doctors and surgeons and greatly appreciated by the wounded men. Pictures of these nuns in the Adams County Historical Society show them wearing wide, starched white bonnets that fitted closely around the face, and long, heavy habits, all of which must have been very uncomfortable in the heat and close quarters. Because of the shortage of space in the town, all fourteen nuns had to sleep in a small space on the floor of a hotel lobby.[10]

Cornelia Hancock, a quiet twenty-three-year-old unmarried Quaker from New Jersey, surprised her family by going to Gettysburg to alleviate the suffering of the wounded. Although she had no nursing skills, she was able to help men write letters and assisted in the distribution of food. After her courageous work was finished, she said, "I shall never be horrified at anything . . . I could stand by and see a man's head taken off, and not be bothered."[11] Mary Cadwell Fisher from nearby York, Pennsylvania, noted that she felt like a surrogate mother to the men, many of whom had to be spoon-fed, like infants. In an article written for the *Philadelphia Weekly Times* twenty years after the battle, she described the field hospital in which she worked: "In all that ghastly array of human misery, between three and four hundred men, there was not one whole individual. . . . Every one had lost an arm or a leg, and in some cases, both . . . What horribly mutilated faces looked up at us from the straw-littered boards, which formed the only beds! No pillows to support bruised and aching head, no blanket to cover shivering limbs. As we entered, the first words . . . were: 'Thank God, there is a woman!. . . . Where did you come from? . . . How did you get here? . . . What did you come for?'"[12]

J. Howard Wert, a young man living on the outskirts of Gettysburg, recorded his observations in articles for local newspapers. One of these told of the generosity of a black woman from Gettysburg named Lydia Smith (not to be confused with Lydia Hamilton Smith, the black woman from Gettysburg who was the common-law wife of abolitionist leader and U.S. Senator Thaddeus Stevens). Wert described Mrs. Smith as belonging "to a despised and down-trodden race, for she was a colored woman."[13] He added that she was poor, but had saved a little money, with which she hired a horse and wagon and drove throughout the surrounding towns, seeking donations of food and clothing for the wounded men on the battlefield. When farmers demanded money for these goods, she paid with her own meager savings. Once her wagon was filled to capacity, she went to the hospitals and the battlefield, the old horse swaying as she walked by its side, distributing items to Union and Confederate soldiers as well. According to Wert, "That noble colored woman saw not in the latter the warriors who were striving to perpetuate the slavery of her race. She saw only the suffering humanity."[14]

During those days following the battle, Victor Chambers's mother was no doubt anxious about where she would give birth. Those who observed her probably looked right through her, for she was "invisible" to them—just another member of that "despised and down-trodden race." There was no room in any of the hospitals crowded with sick and dying soldiers, and no one in the town whom she could approach for help. By July 7, the day of her baby's birth, she found herself in an inhospitable, ravaged place.

Eliza Farnham, who had been visiting from California when the battle erupted, wrote to a friend in Santa Cruz, describing the conditions that prevailed on July 7. "Such sights and conditions! . . . The whole town . . . is one vast hospital. . . . The road, for long distances, is in many places strewn with dead horses. . . . The earth in the roads and fields is ploughed to a mire by the army wheels and horses. . . . [There are] avenues of white tents . . . But, good God, what those quiet-looking tents contained! What spectacles awaited us on the slopes of the rolling hills around us! It is absolutely inconceivable . . . ! Dead and dying, and wounded, ... torn to pieces in every way! . . . the most horrifying thing was to see those limbs lying in front of the surgeon's tent."[15]

This is the world into which Victor Chambers would soon be born. When shortly before his birth his mother at last lifted her heavy body onto an abandoned army wagon, above the muck and mire of the field, she may have found a squatting position most comfortable, since it would ease the pressure on her stomach. This gutted wagon was probably the most solid, secure place she could find for the birth of her child. Many years later, Victor Chambers would speak proudly of the determination of his mother, who endured such loneliness and pain in this blighted and sorrowful place, in order to bring him into the world.

> I was born on the battlefield of Gettysburg July 7th 1863, 4 days after the fight. I was born in an old army wagon that had all the wheels shot off it and the 6 mules were lying in the harness just as they had been killed.
>
> No doctors, no marble slabs, no hot water, no medicines, no one but <u>God</u> and my mother.

Despite the toll that this ordeal must have taken on her body, Victor's mother was probably able to transcend it all, knowing that she had just achieved her greatest victory, giving birth to a child who would grow up in freedom. To celebrate this most life-affirming act, her West African ancestors would have anointed the new baby's head and feet with sacred oils, and whispered a secret name into the baby's ear to protect it from harm in the future. She, too, may have given the baby a name it would keep at least until she was sure he would survive. At the end of the day, she could finally rest and gaze once more at the North Star that had guided her thus far to freedom and victory.

In describing his birth, Victor also noted:

> I was born near the place where Longstreet cut through Sickles' line at the Peach Orchard.

Although neither Victor nor his mother was likely aware of this fact, the place where Longstreet's men cut through Sickles's line is in the same general area where William Barksdale, "Young Massa Will," was fatally wounded by Union troops.

"No more weary travelin'"

[T]he spirit spoke to me,
And said "Rise, my child, your children
And you too shall be free."
Now no more weary travelin' . . .
                                    —*Slave song*

11

After all she had endured and accomplished over the past weeks and months, Victor Chambers's mother had two remaining tasks ahead: to find a place to rest before moving on to Philadelphia, and to chose a name for her son. During the days immediately following the battle, newspapers in Gettysburg, Harrisburg, and Chambersburg carried the same headline in large, bold print: "Victory At Gettysburg! Victory At Gettysburg!" Perhaps this inspired her choice of name for her son Victor. Also, the name "Victoire" was very prevalent among the refugees arriving in Philadelphia from Saint Domingue in the late eighteenth century; it is possible that someone in her family bore that name. In any event, "Victor" was an appropriate name to celebrate both the Union army victory and her own victory over adversity. Victor's middle initial of "D" may have represented a family surname, perhaps that of his maternal grandparents. Victor bore his mother's own surname of Chambers.

By the time she had rested sufficiently and was ready to move on to Chambersburg, she may have found the Underground Railroad contacts she had been seeking earlier in Gettysburg. Basil Biggs, for example, had returned to Gettysburg and could arrange transportation to get her to Chambersburg. He and other Underground Railroad

101

agents, such as the Dobbin family or Maggie Palm, could have arranged needed identification papers and documentation. Without such papers, travel in that part of Pennsylvania was dangerous for runaway slaves. Former slave James Curry, who had run away from a North Carolina plantation, evidently without proper documentation, was told by a woman shortly after his arrival in Chambersburg: "I don't know but you came from Virginia or Maryland, and sometimes, our colored friends come there hither, and think they are free, but the people about here are very ugly, and take them and carry them back; and if you haven't sufficient free papers, I would advise you not to stay here."[1]

For those supported by Underground Railroad agents, however, Chambersburg was a welcoming beacon of hope. Slaves coming from as far away as Maryland could see in the distance the light on the top of Mount Parnell, the highest point in Chambersburg, which let them know that their destination was in sight. To reach Philadelphia from Gettysburg, Chambersburg to the west was actually the best route for safe passage. There, Underground Railroad conductors regularly obtained tickets for travel on the Cumberland Valley Railroad, which was established in 1831 and extended as far south as Virginia and what is now West Virginia. Passengers could travel from Chambersburg, through Carlisle, and ultimately to Harrisburg, where other agents would arrange passage to Philadelphia on the Pennsylvania Railroad.[2] While escaped slaves were waiting in Chambersburg for tickets, documentation papers, or the safest time to move, there were many caves and quarries in which to hide; some of these were located underneath the town itself. In fact, it was in one of these old quarries that Frederick Douglass had met with John Brown shortly before Brown's ill-fated raid at Harper's Ferry (something Douglass urged Brown not to do).

Once in Harrisburg, there were well-established Underground Railroad connections to Philadelphia. One of the important Harrisburg agents was Joseph C. Bustill, a teacher and grandson of a former slave, who would send fugitive slaves onward to fellow agents in Philadelphia, such as his brothers Charles and James, or to William Still, secretary of the Philadelphia Vigilance Committee. Charles and his wife, Emily, also were members of the Vigilance Committee. (Charles and Emily's daughter, who later married an escaped slave named William Drew Robeson, one day would become the mother of the great singer and activist Paul Robeson.) Before they left Harrisburg, Joseph Bustill provided runaways with tickets and forged papers and disguises, if necessary.[3]

Still's records of his clandestine activities, published later in his comprehensive book on the Underground Railroad, contained several references to communications sent to him by Bustill from Harrisburg regarding the transport of people to Philadelphia. One such message noted that Bustill had placed people on the Lightning Train, leaving Harrisburg at 1:30 a.m. and arriving in Philadelphia at 5:00 p.m.[4] Lunsford Lane, a fugitive slave who arrived in Philadelphia via this same train route in 1862, declared upon his arrival: "I stepped my foot on the free land of Philadelphia. It was on the 26th of April [about nine o'clock]. I had the happiness to imagine I heard the shackles fall. . . . I (had) not a dollar in my pocket, yet I think there is not one . . . who (felt) richer or happier than I."[5]

In one of his letters, Victor referred to Philadelphia as his "home city," which he visited in order to place flowers on the graves of his mother and grandmother. Earlier in her life, his grandmother had moved from Philadelphia "to the country," specifically to Smyrna, Delaware, where her daughter, Henrietta Chambers, had been born a year after the abduction of Victor's mother. Just when the elder Mrs. Chambers returned to Philadelphia is not mentioned in the letters, but it might have been after her husband's death or the departure of her daughter Henrietta. Another motivating factor for her return may well have been the worsening living conditions for black people in Delaware. By the 1850s, life for free blacks as well as slaves had become increasingly restrictive. At that time, the state of Delaware passed harsh laws restricting the movement and freedoms of black people. One such ruling made it illegal for a black person to be unemployed, while another authorized the state to sell any such person into slavery or indentured servitude; yet another law allowed authorities to sell African-American children into bondage.[6] These frightful laws and restrictions may well have convinced the elder Mrs. Chambers to leave Delaware and return to her home city of Philadelphia, if she had not already done so. Here, Victor's grandmother would live to a great old age, comforted by the presence of the daughter stolen from her thirty-seven years earlier, and the grandson she must have been thrilled to encounter.

Once she finally made her way back home, Victor's mother likely would have made contact with members of the Vigilance Committee who, with the assistance of local churches and other support groups, would be best able to locate her mother. She must have been anxious to gaze into her mother's eyes again, and yet fearful that her mother might not recognize her. One can imagine the first tentative steps toward recognition—perhaps by mentioning old names or familiar phrases—followed by the realization that each had finally found the other. This long-dreamed-of reunion between mother and daughter must surely have been marked by tears and shouts of joy. It is easy to imagine Victor's mother exclaiming in the words of the old spiritual: "Just look at the shape I'm in! I've been in the storm so long!"

The words of other slaves reunited with family members after years of separation give some insight into what it must have been like for Victor's mother and grandmother. In June 1852, the Canadian abolitionist newspaper *Voice of the Fugitive* printed the words of former slave James Smith, describing the reunion with his wife after an absence of seventeen years. Mr. Smith said he "approached her with trembling," lest he might be mistaken; he then offered his hand and "ventured to call her by her former name, to which she answered with astonishment. At this moment, her eyes sparkled and flashed like strikes of lightening . . . and with uplifted hands and joyful heart exclaimed from the depths of her soul: Oh! Is this my beloved husband, whom I never again expected to see?" The two then embraced and wept aloud for joy.[7]

The seventy-six-year-old Mrs. Chambers must have wept while hearing her daughter's stories of her life as a slave, her escape and arrival in Gettysburg, and the terrible ordeal of that three-day battle. The older woman, in turn, probably told her daughter of events in Philadelphia during that period, and how the black community, fearful of the dire consequences for them of a southern victory, rallied to support the Union army effort. The night before Victor's birth at Gettysburg, Philadelphia was the site of an impressive mass meeting to exhort young black men to join the military effort. The rally, held at the Union League, was marked by bands playing patriotic songs and speeches by enthusiastic orators, including Frederick Douglass.[8]

By the time that the mother, daughter, and new baby began their new life in Philadelphia, they would find that city an unwelcoming, and almost hostile, environment. The city of Philadelphia had changed greatly since the beginning of the nineteenth century, when there was so much vibrancy and hope in the black community. Victor's grandmother would have witnessed a complete disintegration of the community she had known as a child. Earlier in the century, the majority of skilled craftsmen were black—mostly immigrants from the West Indies, like his great-grandparents. The strong monopoly that black families held in Philadelphia's catering business declined sharply with the advent of major hotels with restaurants that could serve large numbers of people. The new hotel owners also favored white employees, to the detriment of black workers, even though the latter were at that time more experienced and skilled in

Race riot in 1849 at California House, 6th & St. Mary's Streets, Philadelphia

the preparation and presentation of food. Resentment of whites toward the black population, which was starting to manifest itself earlier in the century, had risen dramatically by the mid-point of the century. Frederick Douglass said in 1862, "There is not perhaps anywhere to be found a city in which prejudice against color is more rampant than in Philadelphia"[9] which, at that time, had the largest black population of any American city.

By the 1860s, every aspect of life was segregated in Philadelphia— schools, churches, concerts. Those streetcars that accepted black riders made them ride on the outside platforms. Abolitionist rallies were marred by violence, rock-throwing, and torching.

Whereas in the early part of the nineteenth century blacks had constituted a large percentage of the skilled labor force, blacks now made up less than 2 percent of that work force, and only 12 percent of the unskilled labor force. In Philadelphia and elsewhere, employers were fined for hiring black workers.[10] Despite the end of the Civil War and emancipation with all its bright promises, black artisans and skilled workers such as carpenters and caulkers were threatened with the loss of their trades.

The Bureau of Refugees, Freedmen and Abandoned Lands, better known as the Freedmen's Bureau, and other similar organizations such as the Freedmen's Aid Society, were essentially useless and short-lived. With their demise went the hopes of many blacks of obtaining official recognition of their right to work, to live safely, and to be free of coercion by former plantation masters seeking to reestablish control over a cheap labor force.

Within this restrictive environment, Victor's mother and grandmother had to find some way to survive and to raise Victor. Domestic work—taking in washing or sewing in their own home, or working in employers' homes—may have been the only option for them. Like many others, they may also have taken in lodgers to help to supplement their income. Their diet would not have been much better than what Victor's mother had known as a slave. For many poor families, it would usually consist of tea and bread for breakfast, with supper as the only main meal with some protein. Food would be bought in small quantities, whenever money was available. To help poor fami-

lies survive the winter months, "soup houses" were set up throughout the city.[11]

Many black families lived in crowded tenements, mainly situated
in the neighborhoods surrounding Saint Thomas and Mother Bethel
churches, which had played such an important role decades earlier in
the birth of a vibrant black community. The most that any educated,
hardworking black man could aspire to was employment as a porter
or waiter. Work was hard to find, and many black men became
depressed. For a black woman alone, the situation was even more
bleak. Although Victor's mother was finally free and reunited with
her mother, her standard of living was probably not much better than
it had been during her years in bondage.

Victor's formal education in the Philadelphia public schools would
have been for the most part inadequate, assuming that he attended
the public schools. (There are unfortunately no public or parochial
school records for that period, nor is there any record of Victor
Chambers having attended private schools, such as the Colored
Institute for Youth.) Under the Pennsylvania school act of 1854, districts with twenty or more black students remained segregated, while
those with fewer than twenty could integrate. Also, if there were no
separate schools for blacks, the regular schools would have to admit
black children. This meant that in Philadelphia, with its large black
population and already existing separate schools, virtually all education would remain segregated. Schools for black children were usually badly equipped and in poor repair, and it was hard to find either
black or white teachers. Those white teachers who taught in black
schools would often be ostracized by their peers and denied future
employment in the school system. By age fourteen, half of the city's
school-age children had left school and entered the work force.[12]

In 1876, the year of Victor Chambers' thirteenth birthday, the
city of Philadelphia was the site of the great Centennial Exposition
marking the nation's hundredth anniversary. The nation's former
capital was the focal point for the national celebration, which was
characterized by much self-congratulatory rhetoric on the need for
national unity in the wake of a devastating Civil War. Unfortunately,
the celebration paid little attention to role played by African-

Americans in either the history of Philadelphia or that of the nation as a whole.

Ironically, the Centennial Exposition coincided with a period in which black Philadelphians were beginning to focus on the need to preserve their own unique history and legacy. Many African-American veterans groups, literary societies, and historical preservation groups were formed or reconstituted during that era. Black people were becoming increasingly aware of the difficulties in affirming their American citizenship while at the same time acknowledging their African heritage.

At a time when 7 percent of the city's black population was unemployed, no black workers had been hired to work on the Exposition. Furthermore, black people were frequently insulted or assaulted as they entered the Exposition grounds. During the opening ceremonies, Frederick Douglass was allowed to sit on the platform but was not invited to speak. Exposition planners made one token gesture toward the city's black community in granting the request by the Bethel A.M.E. Church to include a bronze statue of its founder, Richard Allen, for display at the event. (This statue later "disappeared").

The only part of the Exposition where there was any meaningful black representation was the section devoted to the arts. There was a sculpture by an Austrian artist depicting the emancipation of a slave. Black sculptor Edmonia Lewis, then residing in Rome, won a medal for one of her works displayed at the Exposition. There were also paintings by black artists such as Robert Duncanson and Edward Mitchell Bannister, who in fact won the highest award for painting at the Exposition.[13]

The fact that Bannister was an African-American was celebrated in Philadelphia's black community and newspapers, which recounted Bannister's earlier work as an abolitionist in Boston, as well as his artistic success. Shortly after President Lincoln had officially allowed black men to serve in the Union army, Edward Bannister and his wife, Christiana Carteaux Bannister, led the effort to obtain equal pay for these soldiers, whom the government in Washington planned to grant smaller salaries than white soldiers. The Bannisters enlisted the aid of wealthy and influential friends in Boston to organize a large fair at which valuable articles and works of art would be sold to raise enough money to pay the difference in salary between white soldiers and those in the newly created black Massachusetts Fifty-fourth Regiment. The publicity raised by this fair, supported by many prominent Boston citizens, sufficed to put pressure on the U.S. Congress to equalize the pay for black and white units. When the Fifty-fourth was ready to be sent off to war, Massachusetts Governor John Andrews asked Christiana Carteaux Bannister to present the regiment's colors to the unit. Edward Bannister also painted a portrait of Robert Gould Shaw, who commanded the Fifty-fourth Regiment. (That painting, which hung in the State House in Boston for many years, later "disappeared.")[14]

Bannister's victory in the painting competition came as a result of that contest's being kept completely anonymous, with titles of the paintings and names of the artists hidden from the judges. Bannister, who at that time was living in Providence, Rhode Island, arrived in Philadelphia to learn that his painting—entitled "Under the Oaks," but listed only as "Number 54" in the anonymous judging—had been awarded the first-prize medal. As he entered the room where the judging had taken place, Bannister said: "There was a great crowd there ahead of me. As I jostled them, many resented my presence, some actually commenting . . . 'What is that colored person in here for?' Finally, when I succeeded in reaching the desk where inquiries were made, I endeavored to gain the attention of the official in charge. . . . Without raising his eyes, he demanded in the most exasperating tone of voice, 'Well, what do you want here anyway?'" Bannister reiterated that he wanted to ascertain whether painting Number 54 was indeed the first-prize medal winner. He declared deliberately, "I am interested in the report that 'Under the Oaks' has received a prize. I painted the picture." In Bannister's words, "an explosion could not have made a more marked impression" on the others in the room.[15]

Reports of Bannister's success must have made a great impression on Victor Chambers, who, like other curious young black people, may well have attended the Exposition despite the difficulties involved. For young people of Victor's generation, Bannister's winning of this prize represented their first exposure to public recognition of a successful African-American. A few years later, Victor would display his own paintings in public. Whether he began painting before hearing of Bannister's success is not known. But it could well have been what inspired him to begin painting, which he may also have viewed as a way to rise above the living conditions and prejudices surrounding him. Within a few years, following his move from Philadelphia to West Chester, Victor Chambers would receive modest public recognition for his artistic work. Perhaps not just coincidentally, he would some years later be living in Providence, not far from Bannister's studio.

"At the closed gate of justice"

[Is it] possible for a man to be both a Negro and an American, without being cursed and spit upon by his fellows, without having the doors of Opportunity closed roughly in his face?
—W. E. B. DuBois, *The Souls of Black Folk*

Like that of other young black men of his generation, Victor Chambers's formal education probably ended when he was about fourteen years old. His mother, however, ensured that Victor was well informed about the Civil War, especially the Battle of Gettysburg. Although Victor said that she gave lectures regarding her experience at Gettysburg, despite intensive research and the assistance of knowledgeable historians and curators at the Library of Congress and several Philadelphia libraries, special collections, and historical societies, I have not been able to find any corroboration of the speech at the Philadelphia Academy of Music referred to in the letters. Unfortunately, that institution's archival holdings are restricted to playbills and other material concerning musical productions only, although the Academy was often used for political rallies and addresses by Union army officers, abolitionists and others. Without a firm date for the lecture, it has been virtually impossible to find any reference to that event—despite searches in Philadelphia newspapers and the personal papers of all those described as present on the stage with Victor Chambers's mother for that particular lecture. The letters also state that Victor's mother took him to the Gettysburg battlefield.

> I have been to Gettysburg with mother 4 times and she has pointed out the places where men were piled 10 high at the Bloody Angle and Devil's Den.

Victor Chambers's pride in his mother comes through clearly in his letters. The passion with which he speaks of the Union cause reveals the powerful impression his mother must have made upon her son and others who attended her lectures. That passion can be detected not only in the words he used, but also in his use of underlining and exclamation marks. In addressing Michael Carroll, he wrote:

> If I was a respected Union Soldier, as I know <u>you</u> are, while there was a rebel soldier wearing the gray in Dixie, I would <u>never</u> acknowledge him as my equal as a "Veteran", wearing the uniform of <u>the C.S.A.</u>
>   No Sir
>   <u>Never Never Never.</u>

> I feel, and as my Mother said to me oh so often, that <u>every</u> [word underlined twice] Colored American owes a deabt [sic] of gratitude <u>forever</u> [word underlined twice and encircled] to the veteran soldiers of the Grand Army of the Republic.

> I was at Gettysburg on her 50th anniversary of the battle 1913. I heard that old rebel yell when they made the supposed charge across the wheat field against the Union left center. They hated you in '63. They hate you now.

His devotion to his mother is evident in the fact that he never used the simple past tense in speaking of her, although she would have been long dead by the time that Victor wrote his letters in 1931, when he was sixty-seven. He usually used either present ("Mother tells me"), or perfect tense ("Mother has told me").

Victor stated that his grandmother died in 1884, at the age of ninety-seven, when he would have been twenty-one years old. Census records show that Victor was living in West Chester in the late 1880s. In light of his great love and admiration for his mother, it seems unlikely that he would have left Philadelphia while she was still alive. She could well have died about the same time as her mother. The letters state that both women were buried in Philadelphia.

Despite his great devotion to his mother, Victor Chambers must have wondered throughout his life about the identity of his father. Like Frederick Douglass and other men born to slaves, however, he likely had too much respect for his mother to ever make inquiries into this difficult issue. He was no doubt eager to solve the mystery of his parentage, but at the same time wary that it might turn out to be that which he most feared. Frederick Douglass expressed those same fears and doubts. He wrote, "I say nothing of father, for he is shrouded in a mystery I have never been able to penetrate. Slavery does away with fathers. . . . The name of the child is not expected to be that of the father. . . . It was sometimes whispered that my master was my father."[1]

Besides the deaths of his mother and grandmother, there were probably many other reasons for Victor's decision to leave Philadelphia. By the late 1880s, when he was in his mid-twenties, he was perhaps alone for the first time and ready to know more about himself and the world, as well as to expand his freedom of choice and development as a person. In addition, the atmosphere in Philadelphia was becoming increasingly more restricting for young black men, for whom very few options were available.

Victor's choice of West Chester was an especially good one for him at that time, in that it provided a welcome escape from the increasing racial polarization in Philadelphia. Just twenty-three miles west of Philadelphia, West Chester had been founded by Quakers and was proud of its racial tolerance. It had been a major Underground Railroad stop and boasted an energetic, growing African-American middle class that had begun to flourish in the 1850s, when the black population of 452 was a relatively small percentage of the total population of 3,172 inhabitants. By the 1890s, the African-American population had increased to almost one-fourth the total population of approximately 10,000 inhabitants. Just as in Philadelphia in the early part of the century, black entrepreneurs in West Chester acquired wealth and status for themselves in the catering and restaurant business. These businesses, however, did not suffer the decline experienced by black-owned enterprises in Philadelphia.[2]

The wealthy black entrepreneurs of West Chester did not remain aloof from the less prosperous members of their community. They were active in the Bethel A.M.E. and Second Presbyterian churches, where they sponsored literary discussions, art competitions, and political debates. These civic-minded wealthy black residents saw themselves not as members of an elite class, but rather as mentors and public servants helping to educate and support their own community.[3]

West Chester provided other networking and support centers for young African-Americans; among these, the Knights Templar and the Free and Accepted Masons. Another influential and vibrant group was the Liberty Cornet Band, which counted many of the community's wealthy black businessmen among its members.[4] From the late 1870s to about 1890, the pastor of the Bethel A.M.E. Church was a man named Lewis C. Chambers (no known relation to Victor), who was a driving force in the black community. Under his stewardship, the Bethel church became the largest black congregation in West Chester. The Reverend Chambers's well-known revivals converted scores of people and brought new members to his church, which Chambers saw as "a perpetuation of the ideals of brotherhood of man expressed by Richard Allen," the influential founder of Philadelphia's first A.M.E. church, which was a vital force in the development of Philadelphia's black community earlier in the century.[5] Church records show that Victor Chambers was a member of West Chester's Bethel A.M.E. Church.

West Chester was also a strong Republican Party stronghold, whose two local newspapers, the *Daily Local News* and *Morning Republican*, were controlled by the party, and where employment opportunities depended in large part on one's party affiliation. The Republican Party knew it could count on the support of the local black community, although this support weakened over the years as the party increasingly neglected the demands of that constituency. Pressure by black voters to be taken into account by local political leaders resulted in the election of a black man to the borough council in 1882; that seat remained in the hands of black council members until 1892. During the 1880s and 1890s, the African-American community of West Chester became increasingly vocal in protesting school segregation, with many threatening to leave the Republican Party over this issue. This dispute, however, remained deadlocked for decades to come. Younger members of the community, impatient with the slow rate of progress, formed the Independent Republican Colored Club to demonstrate that they were a force to be reckoned with.[6] Despite these voices of protest, there were no large-scale defections from the Republican Party until the 1930s.

Because the South continued to be identified with the Democratic Party, Victor Chambers most likely remained faithful to the Republican Party. This likelihood is reinforced by the type of work that he obtained in West Chester, as porter in one of the town's most prestigious firms. Jobs of that nature were usually reserved for black men who remained strong Republican Party loyalists. The T. T. Smith Tobacco Company was a major enterprise whose influence extended throughout the country, from the large East Coast cities to the developing West. Local directories for the early 1890s show Victor Chambers working as a porter for the T. T. Smith Company at 10 and 12 East Gay Street, and living in a boardinghouse just around the corner, at 27 South High Street.[7] Both of these buildings remain in existence today.

In 1872, when T. T. Smith opened its newly expanded and renovated location on Gay Street, just opposite the Green Tree Inn and Hotel, the whole town was invited to tour the luxuriously appointed store, with its gleaming oak panels and staircase, and silver-mounted glass show cases. Townspeople marveled at the street-front show windows, where a large mirrorlike reflector, attached to three gas jets, illumined almost the entire street at night. On opening day, Smith served free drinks to gentlemen, and in the evening the establishment hosted a concert for the town by the African-American Liberty Cornet Band.[8] In 1879, the entire town's imagination was captured by the fact that Smith had installed a telephone line between his home and the store.[9]

With more than seventy employees involved in the manufacture of cigars at a separate plant in Marshallton (run by Smith's brother), Smith became the sole supplier to major hotels and theaters throughout Pennsylvania. The company also had agents working for it in New York, Alabama, the "Montana territories," and other points in the west.[10] In 1890, the T. T. Smith store on Gay Street installed glass pavement lights, ensuring its continuation as the most impressive establishment in West Chester.[11]

After having secured what was considered a plum job for a young black man, Victor Chambers must have been excited about working for such an impressive company. This was just the type of place for a young man to establish his new identity, and he was in a position to be noticed and, no doubt, admired by young women of the town. Andrew J. Bell, who knew Victor Chambers later in life, described him as a tall, impressive man, with a large frame but not overweight, and with a gregarious personality. Mr. Bell told me that Victor Chambers made an immediate, positive impact on others. He had a round face and an amiable smile and was very fastidious about his appearance. His moustache was neatly trimmed and slightly curled at the ends. Mr. Bell added that Victor's skin was a true brown, the color of warm, polished wood. He also mentioned that women found Victor very attractive and that he was at ease in their company and obviously enjoyed their attention.

Not long after his arrival in West Chester, Victor received the first, albeit small-scale, public recognition for his work as an artist. At a December 1888 art exposition sponsored by the Bethel A.M.E. Church, Victor won first prize for a drawing (not further identified).[12] A few years later, the *Daily Republican* reported, "Victor D. Chambers, West Chester, who is known to be handy with the crayon, has added another piece of work to his collection. It can be seen in the window at the office of Dr. F. M. Freeman, where it is much admired. The scene presented is a horse's head, while in front of this is a pedestal upon which a dog is lying, the whole showing that Mr. Chambers possesses much skill in crayon work."[13] The Chester County Art Association, which unfortunately could find no record of Victor's work, explained that the word "crayon," as used in those days, refers to pastels and/or charcoal.

On January 25, 1897, a newspaper article noted that "Victor D. Chambers has finished and will place upon exhibition a painting upon which he has labored for some time. The production is entitled "With Her Pets," and the thought and workmanship reflects great credit upon the painter. With Her Pets will be placed on view in one of the windows of Mr. Rosenberg's store. Victor D. Chambers, the artist, is a young colored man in the employ of Thomas T. Smith, and this is not the first time that his work has attracted favorable notice."[14] Later that year, on August 31, 1897, another article reported that: "Victor Chambers, the coachman for T. T. Smith, who is somewhat of an artist, shipped a couple of pictures to Boston, Mass. yesterday. Both were fine pieces of work, and reflect considerable credit on his ability as an artist. He is engaged in another one at present."[15]

Sometime during his stay in West Chester, Victor Chambers reached another important benchmark in his life. Here he met and married a young woman named Anna Cole, born in West Chester in 1868, the daughter of Isaac and Caroline Cole, who were born in Maryland. Mr. Cole was a veteran of the Civil War.[16] It is likely that the marriage was brought about through Anna's brother, Isaac Cole, Jr., who worked as a hostler at the Green Tree Inn, directly across the street from the T. T. Smith Company on Gay Street.[17] Since the younger Isaac, born in 1861, and Victor were about the same age and working near one another in similar jobs, it is logical that they would have become acquainted. The fact that Isaac's father had fought in the Civil War may also have piqued Victor's interest in getting to know the Cole family.

Victor may also have been attracted to Anna because she had a young son, Oscar.[18] While some men may not have looked favorably on inheriting a ready-made family, Victor may well have seen in the young unwed mother and her son a reflection of himself and his cherished mother. In marrying Anna Cole, Victor would take on two important roles that had been lacking in his own family life; namely, that of husband and father.

Toward the end of the 1890s, life for black residents of West Chester changed for the worse. The fortunes of wealthy African-Americans in the catering and restaurant businesses saw a sharp decline, similar to that which had occurred in Philadelphia a couple of generations earlier. As newly arrived European—mainly Irish and German—immigrants moved into the area, racially motivated attacks against African-Americans rose dramatically.[19] In 1898, Victor and Anna Chambers moved to Rhode Island. Since there are no records of Oscar Cole having moved to Rhode Island with his mother and step-father, he may well have been old enough to begin his own life at that time. (Sometime in the early 1900s, Oscar moved to New Jersey.)

Besides the worsening social conditions, Victor may have had other reasons for moving to Rhode Island. Joseph Holland Banks, who was married to the sister of Victor's mother, lived in Providence where, as a former member of the Rhode Island legislature, he might have been well placed to assist his nephew. Providence was also home to the artist Edward M. Bannister, whose success at the Philadelphia Centennial Exposition in 1876 may well have been the catalyst for Victor's own interest in art.

"If it were not for men like you, I would be in slavery"

13

To be a Negro in a day like this
Demands strange loyalty. We serve a flag
Which is to us white freedom's emphasis.
—*James David Corothers,*
"At the Closed Gate of Justice"

In 1898, Victor and Anna Chambers, aged thirty-five and thirty years respectively, arrived in the city of Providence, which in no way represented a welcome haven for African-Americans. Their disappointment must have been similar to that described by William J. Brown in his 1883 autobiography. Mr. Brown, who was a leader and chronicler of Providence's African-American community in the latter half of the nineteenth century and whose family had been slaves of Moses Brown, spoke in his memoir of the "discouragement and disadvantage" of being a black person in Providence, and of the "tortuous pace" of progress toward equality and justice.[1] (Moses Brown was a wealthy manufacturer, slave owner turned abolitionist, and uncle of the man for whom Brown University was named.[2])

Nevertheless, large numbers of African-Americans left the South in the late 1890s and early 1900s for this northern city, which in many ways showed them nothing but hostility. When Victor Chambers arrived in Providence, he found employment at a cigar and tobacco shop on Cranston Street, perhaps with the help of a recommendation from the T. T. Smith Tobacco Company, where he had worked while in West Chester. Although Providence was becoming one of the

largest industrial centers in the country, access to jobs in the booming textile, machine tool, and jewelry factories was denied to people
such as Victor Chambers.

Providence had one of the most corrupt municipal political systems in the country, and the Rhode Island legislature was led by a
small group of Republican politicians who were totally under the
control of influential factory owners.[3] Immigrants from Europe were
pouring into the city to work in the mills and factories—so much so
that, by 1900, seven out of ten residents of Providence were foreign-
born.[4] While thousands of factory jobs were offered to these immigrants, African-Americans were denied similar opportunities. Rather,
they remained limited to menial jobs such as porters, carpenters,
laundresses, teamsters, and house painters. Even those few African-
Americans who amassed some wealth could not aspire to be more
than manual laborers; there were no black professionals or entrepreneurs. Although blacks and whites often lived in the same neighborhood, every other aspect of life was segregated; black people had to
use separate theaters, hotels, restaurants, and railroad cars.[5]

Like their counterparts in Philadelphia, black people in Providence
formed important organizations to aid and strengthen their own
community. Groups such as Masonic Lodges, the African Union
Society, the Mutual Relief Society, and the Female Literary Society,
among others, were established throughout the city. Just as in
Philadelphia, the city's black churches were very influential and sup-
portive. Thanks to the efforts of these churches and their related
schools, almost half of Providence's black population was literate by
the late 1880s. Among the black community's places of worship were
the African Union Meeting House (later known as the Meeting Street
Baptist Church), the Pond Street Baptist Church (also known as the
Second Freewill Baptist Church), the Winter Street A.M.E. Zion
Church, and Christ Episcopal Church.[6] The Pond Street Baptist
Church, in particular, served as a vibrant center for black intellectu-
als and regularly sponsored musical programs, literary discussion
groups, and other programs that afforded a unique opportunity for
young people in the community to interact with African-American
students from Brown University and its women's college, Pembroke.

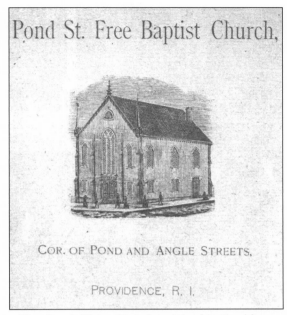

Pond St. Free Baptist Church,

COR. OF POND AND ANGLE STREETS,

PROVIDENCE, R. I.

The church Victor Chambers joined in Providence

It was this church that Victor Chambers joined shortly after his arrival in Providence —even though his wife, Anna, and his uncle, Joseph H. Banks, attended the Winter Street A.M.E. Zion Church.

While Victor was still living in Philadelphia with his mother and grandmother, they must certainly have corresponded with, or perhaps been visited by, Henrietta Chambers Banks, who surely would have wanted to meet the sister she had never known. Henrietta died in Providence in 1895; just a year after Victor's move to Providence, her husband died suddenly of a stroke. Victor had probably hoped that his well-connected uncle could provide useful contacts for him, as well as insights into his mother's family and her life on the Barksdale plantation. As Victor said in the letters to my great-grandfather:

> My uncle, the late Joseph H. Banks of 101 Grove Street this city[,] and the late James C. LeCount (I guess you knew both of them) were both slaves on the Barksdale plantation.

Both Mr. Banks and Mr. LeCount had been born in Delaware, Mr. Banks in 1827 and Mr. LeCount in 1836. Each had parents with French names (the latter's mother was from the Joland family, while

Photo and notice of Joseph Banks's funeral from the Providence Evening Bulletin, September 6, 1899

Mr. Banks' mother was named Boyer). Perhaps, like Victor's ancestors, they were descended from Haitian refugees. In Philadelphia, there was, in fact, a prominent LeCount family, originally from Haiti, that ran a lucrative catering business. Since both men had been slaves on the Barksdale plantation, they could possibly been kidnapped by slave-catchers belonging to one of the gangs operating in Delaware at the time of Victor's mother's abduction in 1827. It probably did not take long for Victor's mother, who was older than these two boys, to discover how much she had in common with them. Also, since it was customary for older girls to care for younger children on the plantation, she may well have filled that role in their lives. Whether James LeCount and Joseph Banks escaped at the same time from the Barksdale plantation is not known, although each would have left in his teens or early twenties—the average age of most successful runaway slaves.

James LeCount had established himself in Providence by age seventeen. Joseph Banks had made his way to his home state of Delaware in 1849, where, at age twenty-two, he married twenty-one-year old Henrietta Chambers. Joseph Banks's visit to the family of the woman he had known on the plantation not only led to his own marriage but also provided the Chambers family with the welcome news that their other daughter, while still a slave, was nonetheless alive after her abduction twenty-two years earlier.

Because slave-catchers were still operating in Delaware and that state was passing increasingly harsh laws restricting the freedom of free black people, Joseph and Henrietta, along with his parents and their two children, moved to Providence—perhaps at the urging of James LeCount, who had become a well-respected member of the African-American community in Providence. When the Civil War broke out, James LeCount served as a corporal in Rhode Island's Company L, Colored Heavy Artillery. When he died in April 1923, he was the last surviving member of the Ives Post Grand Army of the Republic (GAR) and the oldest member of the King Solomon's Lodge of Masons. Upon his death, the African-American paper, *The Advance*, carried a front-page picture of the eighty-seven-year old veteran in his Civil War uniform. The *Providence Evening Bulletin* of April 28, 1924, also gave prominent coverage to Mr. LeCount's death.[7] Although well known and respected in his own community, the only employment he could obtain in Rhode Island was that of stove repairman. A generation later, when greater strides would be made toward equal opportunity, Mr. LeCount's adopted son, Joseph G. LeCount, became one of the most influential civil rights lawyers and leaders in Rhode Island, responsible for ending segregation in the state's theaters and public establishments.[8]

After their arrival in Providence in 1883, Joseph and Henrietta Chambers Banks would have three more children. During most of his life in Rhode Island, Joseph Banks worked as a carpenter. Despite his low economic status, Mr. Banks became involved in city and state politics. He was elected to a two-year term in the Rhode Island legislature, where he served on the prestigious Education Committee.[9] While most African-Americans remained loyal to the party of Lincoln, others were impatient with the Republican Party's progress in recognizing the value of that support. Joseph H. Banks ultimately broke away and joined the Democratic Party, despite its association with the slaveholding South. His picture, which appeared on the front page of the *Providence Journal* at the time of his death in 1899, reveals the strong jawline and determined look of a man who would not be taken for granted and would be capable of bucking a powerful political establishment.

Victor and Anna Chambers, who lived in the same apartment building on Grove Street in Providence as his uncle, would have attended his impressive funeral, which received prominent attention in all of the city's newspapers. Senior public officials, and people from throughout the city, attended the service at the Winter Street A.M.E. Zion Church. Although scheduled for two-thirty, it did not start until after three o'clock, when the lengthy cortege, accompanied by dirges played by a group identified as the Rhode Island Brass Band, finally made its way to the church. Many tributes were made by clergy from Rhode Island and neighboring Connecticut, who exhorted young men to emulate the life of this distinguished man.

In early 1901, Victor Chambers would learn of the death of another older man he had admired and perhaps emulated in his efforts to establish himself as an artist. Edward Mitchell Bannister, who had won the coveted first prize for painting at the nation's Centennial Exposition in Philadelphia in 1876, died while at prayer in his church on the evening of January 8, 1901.[10] During the years just prior to his death, Bannister's health and mental faculties had failed him, and the public's taste in art had changed, to the detriment of Bannister's artistic reputation. This forceful man had been an influential abolitionist as well as a successful artist. He and his wife, Christiana Carteaux Bannister, were responsible for calling the public's attention to the cause of black soldiers during the Civil War and for seeing that they received the same pay as their white comrades. He and sixteen other artists in Providence had founded the Providence Art Club; this same group was also responsible for the creation of the Rhode Island School of Design.[11]

By the early days of the twentieth century, Bannister's financial and health problems made him increasingly discouraged; he had frequent memory lapses and often became disoriented during his evening strolls. Despite all these difficulties, he completed a landscape that he planned to exhibit on January 10, 1901, which would have been just two days after his death. In November of that year, Bannister's colleagues gathered to decide how best to commemorate their friend's contribution to the arts.

Bannister's friend George W. Whitaker read aloud to the group a letter he had once received from Bannister, in which the artist spoke wistfully about his lack of formal training. In that letter, which appeared in the Providence newspaper, Bannister said, "All that I would do, I cannot; that is, all that I would say in art, simply for want of proper training. With God's help, however, I hope to be able to deliver the message entrusted to me."[12]

In his often brooding landscapes, Bannister had sought to convey some sense of the majesty and power of God. He may also have intended to communicate, through the gloomy, ominous clouds that dominate many of his landscapes, an underlying pessimism about his own future and that of all African-Americans in these years after the Civil War, when progress toward justice and equality still lagged so far behind.

Perhaps, after seeing the decline in Bannister's fortunes and especially after reading the artist's own lament about his lack of formal training, Victor Chambers could see the futility of his pursuing any further work as an artist. There are no records of his joining any art groups or competitions in Providence, as he had done in West Chester. Victor had other pressing concerns that demanded his attention; namely, seeking a better job and perhaps finding some meaningful way to contribute to society.

The powerful Rhode Island Republican Party enjoyed the support of the majority of the state's African-Americans and made continual efforts to retain and recruit members. These included party-sponsored torchlight parades in the predominantly African-American neighborhoods. The parades, accompanied by musical groups, bands, and people carrying signs and chanting slogans, usually ended at a hall or meeting place where Republican candidates made speeches in which they emphasized the link between the Democratic Party and the South.[13] Those who supported such events and worked for the cause of the Republican Party were often rewarded with what were considered plum jobs, including "several jobs sweeping streets and a few jobs as janitors in school buildings."[14] This is evidently the path Victor Chambers chose; by 1910 he had been appointed to one of these sought-after positions. As he mentioned in one of his letters:

> I remember . . . way back in 1910 when I was janitor of Point Street Grammar School.

Coincidentally, the man whom he replaced in his first janitorial position had much in common with Victor and his mother. That man, Armstead Lewis, had been at the Battle of Gettysburg as the body servant to Confederate General John Bell Hood. Like Victor's mother, he had previously been a slave on a plantation in Virginia.[15] He must have been amazed to hear the story of Victor's mother's escape from slavery and her ordeal at Gettysburg.

Victor Chambers, like other black men and women of his generation, had great reverence for those who fought in the Civil War, and saw them as their liberators. In the city of Providence, African-Americans turned out in large numbers on Memorial Day to honor the surviving Civil War veterans. In 1924, a man named Philip Coleman told Works Progress Administration interviewers of his admiration for the men he saw marching in the Memorial Day parade in Providence. Mr. Coleman, who had been a slave in Virginia and later became a stevedore along the Fox Point and India Point waterfronts in Providence, said that when he saw the Union army veterans marching to the cemeteries to honor their deceased comrades, he was aware that they had fought to ensure his freedom. He said, "It was 48 years ago that I came to Providence, and saw for the first time a

Memorial Day observance. I can recall that the procession of men in blue impressed me deeply. The men in that line were of those who went South to fight that I might be free."[16] Those sentiments are the same as those expressed later by Victor Chambers in his letter to my great-grandfather:

> If it had not been for <u>you</u> and thousands like you, <u>I</u> would now be in slavery.

Like Philip Coleman, Victor Chambers probably attended the Memorial Day parades each year to honor the surviving veterans. In July 1913, he attended the fiftieth anniversary of the Battle of Gettysburg, which my great-grandfather also attended. While my great-grandfather made the arduous journey from Providence to Gettysburg at the age of seventy-three to honor fallen comrades and talk with other surviving members of his New York regiment, Victor viewed the event in another light.

> I was at Gettysburg on her 50th anniversary of the battle 1913.

Veterans at the summit of Little Round Top during the Gettysburg reunion

For Victor Chambers, the commemoration was as much "her" (his mother's) anniversary as it was that of the men who fought at Gettysburg.

While my great-grandfather told a newspaper reporter after that reunion that "some of the Johnny Rebs were pretty good fellows," Victor was unable to see the southerners present at the ceremonies as equals to the Union army veterans. He could not forget how the slaveholding South had treated his mother, whose memory he honored by making the trip to Gettysburg that hot July, when weather reports put the temperatures at Gettysburg above one hundred degrees for the duration of the three-day ceremonies. Victor's strong emotions upon seeing the respect paid to Confederate soldiers at the fiftieth reunion came through clearly when he wrote the letters to my great-grandfather some eighteen years later:

> If I was a respected Union soldier as I know you are, while there was a rebel soldier wearing the gray in Dixie, I would never acknowledge him as my equal as a "veteran". . . . No Sir.
> Never never never! . . .
>
> They hated you in '63. They hate you now.

Although Victor did not specify in the letters, I believe it is likely that he would have remained at Gettysburg beyond the closing ceremonies on July 3 in order to be there on July 7, the anniversary of his birth on that battlefield. As he stood on the spot where he was born, surrounded by the many peach trees in that area, Victor was also unconsciously fulfilling a West African custom whereby a man returns on his birthday to the place, usually beneath a fruit-bearing tree, where his mother would have buried the placenta.[17]

During that visit to Gettysburg, Victor would have had time alone to reflect on the course of his life. Now fifty years old, he had not had the opportunity to serve his country or community as had Joseph Banks or James LeCount. Furthermore, with even less training and none of the recognition that Edward Bannister had received, he had to abandon his aspirations to become a painter. While his wife Anna had moved to Providence with him in 1898, they had no children and probably drifted apart over the years; they even worshiped in different churches. Upon Anna's death in Providence in 1943, her obituary read that she was the "divorced wife" of Victor Chambers.[18]

Andrew J. Bell, author of *An Assessment of Life in Rhode Island as an African-American,* told me that it was common practice in those days to divorce "unofficially"; any marriages after that would usually be under "common law" arrangements. Even today, Rhode Island remains one of thirteen states that do not require a formal wedding or marriage ceremony to be legally married, although people do have to go the courts to have a previous divorce finalized.[19]

Just when Victor and Anna divorced and when he met Selena Lincoln is not known, although census records for 1920 show Victor, then age fifty-seven, living with Selena, age fifty-six. Selena's family history is unique: her maternal grandparents were Narragansett Indians of the Wampanaug tribe who had been sent to England so that Queen Victoria could see native Americans firsthand. They remained in London, where their daughter, named Selena, was born. After a failed marriage in England, Selena left for her ancestral home in Rhode Island, where she eventually married Harrison Gray Otis Lincoln. It was from this union that Selena Lincoln, the second wife of Victor Chambers, was born. One of Selena's younger cousins was Nancy Elizabeth Prophet, known as Elizabeth Prophet, a sculptor of mixed African-American and Narragansett Indian heritage.[20] Elizabeth Prophet saved enough money to obtain a degree at the Rhode Island School of Design, which has examples of her work on display today. Because galleries refused to allow her to be present during exhibits of her works—on the grounds that people would not want to purchase work by a woman of color—she left for Paris, where she graduated from the prestigious École des Beaux Arts and won several prizes for sculpture. In the 1930s she returned to the United States, where she taught at Atlanta University and Spelman College. Because of her father's illness, she later returned to Providence. From that time on, her life was marked by unhappiness, poverty (she had to work as a maid), and the sorrow at never receiving recognition in

Sculptor went overseas to gain recognition here

NANCY ELIZABETH PROPHET

While American society frowned upon her pursuing an artistic career, Nancy Elizabeth Prophet succeeded in becoming an acclaimed sculptor in the United States and Europe.

When she could not find artistic acceptance in the United States, Prophet moved to Paris, earned fame and returned to her country.

"She never whined or made any excuses for herself," her friend and supporter W.E.B. DuBois wrote in an article in Crisis magazine. "She never submitted to patronage, cringed to the great or begged of the poor. She worked."

Prophet was born in the village of Arctic, then a part of Warwick, in 1890 to a black mother and a Narragansett Indian father. Because her family was not wealthy, relatives encouraged her to become a domestic worker or a "teacher of her people," because those were the only occupations by which a woman of color could support herself.

In spite of the well-intentioned advice, Prophet kept her goals intact. She worked for four years to save enough mon-

and recognition in the French world, Prophet returned to the United States and found that s[...] had achieved acceptance.

Ten years after the Newpo[...] gallery snubbed her, her artwor[...] was displayed in New York and Rhode Island. She was invited t[...] show her work at the Newport Art Association, where million-aire cottage owners came to se[...] her work.

In 1934, Prophet moved t[...] Atlanta to teach art, first at Atlanta University, then at Spelman College, to give aspirin[...] young black artists the encour-agement she never received.

In the mid-1940s, she re-turned to Providence to care fo[...] her sick father, who lived on Benefit Street. She continued sculpting but spent much time alone and without much mone[...]

Despite her talent and vi-sion, Prophet quietly spent mos[...] of her life mired in unhappiness[...] biographers contend. In Paris, she at times lived with her then[...] husband, Francis Ford, whom she had met at RISD. But those years, while artistically affluent, were spent primarily alone in h[...] studio apartment.

Prophet once said that her education came from "the col[...]

Nancy Prophet, artist and cousin of Victor Chambers's second wife

her home state. Only ten of her sculptures are known to exist today; she destroyed many herself out of anger and frustration.[21]

Victor's knowledge of the treatment given to his wife's cousin, who could receive no recognition for her accomplishments as an artist, must surely have cemented his decision to abandon painting. Victor would remain a janitor in the Providence schools until his death in 1943.

In 1931 he read the account of Michael R. Carroll's Civil War service in the Union army and sent the letters that serve as the basis for this book. My mother, who was usually present whenever Victor visited her grandfather, said that the old veteran was greatly touched by

MICHAEL CARROLL, G. A. R. VET, DEAD

years. He came to this city about 62 years ago and entered the employ of the Gorham Manufacturing Company. Later he was employed by the city for

CLAREN(
FUNE

Father of Harbor Master, Lieutenant in Civil War, Stricken in 93rd Year.

Michael R. Carroll, Lieutenant in the Civil War and father of Harbor Master William H. Carroll, died suddenly last night at his home, 33 Pitman street. He was 92 years old.

Until a few days ago, Mr. Carroll apparently was in good health and had prepared his uniform for appearance with the four surviving members of Bucklin Post, G. A. R., of East Providence, in the Memorial Day procession tomorrow. He had never failed to take part in the annual observance.

Was Head of City Yards

A well-known resident of Fox Point, where he lived more than 40 years, Mr. Carroll had served as superintendent of the City Yards for 25 years prior to his retirement in 1920. He lived on Tockwotton street until forced to move because his house was in the path of the new Fox Point boulevard.

A native of New York, the Civil War veteran enlisted there in February, 1862, at the age of 21 years. He saw active service during more than 3½ years and

The funera
student of g
partment st(
bridge, Mass
morning fro
funeral home
day at his hor
81st year.
A resident
21 years, he
search work i
nounced he
his ancestry (
of his death
historical tre
from earliest
Mr. Shum
Mass., lived
later moved
many years
Johnson-Coll
came to Pro
a member
Knights of F
Surviving
Julia (Chap
Mrs. Ida I.
and a nephe
York.

LODG(
Otho Boon

Michael Carroll's obituary

Victor's pride in his mother and was gratified to learn that his service had played a role in ending the scourge of slavery. Prior to that, he had only some vague realization that he had fought to preserve the Union. Now he had a concrete example, in the person of Victor Chambers, of the value of his contribution.

My mother said that Victor Chambers called her home on May 29, 1933, after having read in the newspaper of her grandfather's death. The headline read, "Michael R. Carroll, G.A.R. Vet, Dead—Lieutenant in Civil War Stricken in 93rd Year"; the obituary continued, "Until a few days ago, Mr. Carroll was apparently in good health, and had prepared his uniform for his appearance in the Memorial Day procession tomorrow. He never failed to take part in the annual observance."[22]

A few days after his favorite holiday had passed, the ninety-three-year old veteran was buried with full military honors. As the body was taken to the grave by a horse-drawn caisson, a haunting sound wafted out over the crowd. At that moment, my mother looked out over the large gathering and, amid all the faces, noticed one man, tall with dark brown skin, with a distinctive well-trimmed mustache, his head uncovered and holding his hat over his heart, as two buglers, one at each end of the cemetery, played "Taps," once known as "Butterfield's Lullaby," the same tune that once played over the sleeping men at Gettysburg.

Nothing is known of Victor Chambers during the remaining decade of his life. There surely must have been more of the "discouragement and disappointment" spoken of many years earlier by William J. Brown. Like Mr. Brown, Victor must have been concerned about his own legacy, as well as the "tortuous pace of progress" toward equality and justice for African-Americans of his generation.[23]

While his mother and thousands of her generation remain nameless, Victor Chambers and his generation left behind records, albeit brief ones, of their births, occupations, and deaths. While not completely anonymous, they remained nonetheless invisible to the majority of those around them, who were unable to see beyond outward appearances to the essential substance, soul, and history of others different from them. Victor Chambers died of heart failure on Christmas Day in 1943, alone in a hospital bed in Providence. Unlike Joseph Banks, James LeCount, Armstead Lewis, or Edward Bannister, his passing would receive no prominent newspaper coverage, nor would there be any large church funeral. Because so few people knew him, a small prayer service, led by the pastor of the Pond Street Baptist Church, was held at the Bell funeral home. Although initially buried in his wife Selena's family plot in Warwick, Victor was reinterred later that year in the Locust Grove Cemetery in Providence.[24] He died in much the same unheralded manner in which he had come into the world: no headlines, no caissons, no dirges or eulogies, no one to recognize his worth: No one but God and his mother.

"Let the kin of the dead come and hold him by the head."

If in the twilight of memory we should meet
once more, we shall speak again together
and you shall sing to me a deeper song.
—*Khalil Gibran, The Prophet*

The previous chapters present the facts known about Victor Chambers and his mother, based on his letters and my own inquiries into each of their lives. My research into the rich history and lore of Dahomey, which could well have been their ancestral homeland, inspired me to imagine what might have transpired after Victor's death on Christmas Day in 1943. The Dahomean burial ritual would seem only fitting for one who honored his mother and forebears as did Victor Chambers.

Victor hears his mother's voice calling him by the secret name she had whispered to him when he was born. He also hears the burial songs of the ancient kingdom of Dahomey and is amazed that he understands the words sung in the Fon language. He also knows that it is night and that the ceremony is for him. Soon, the blessings and rituals reserved for the death of one who had lived honorably will be bestowed on him. The *dokwega*, or priest, will begin the ceremony of the dead, which is also the ceremony of deification, for Victor will now join the company of his ancestors.

Chanting lines of people come forward with gifts for the dead: slaughtered animals, fruit, sacred appliquéd cloths, and beads. Others bring forth gifts for the ancestors: intricately carved calabashes and delicately sculpted figures of wood, gold, silver, and brass. All the people dance in a counterclockwise circle around the edge of the sacred forest. In a clearing facing the sea lies Victor. Before him, under a white umbrella trimmed with appliqué cloth designs, stands the dokwega, who is adorned in multicolored and multistranded anklets, collar necklace, and bracelets made of glass beads and cowrie shells. On his head is a goatskin crown sewn with the same beads and shells.

Tall bronze women covered in gold jewels and flowers surround the dokwega, waving branches. Other women come forward to sweep the purifying broom over Victor's head and body. The women chant softly as young men in colorful cloths accompany them on flutes and drums. The dokwega signals for six strong older men dressed in white to hold up the body, while he intones:

> We have arrived to transport the body,
> The children of Djegbwe take thee,
> And into the sea thou wilt fall.[1]

Suddenly, a star falls into the sea, and those present know that Victor's spirit has begun its journey to join the *vodun*, the deified ancestors. As the men place the body on a bed strewn with sacred leaves and transport it to the straw-covered ancestral hut, the dokwega calls to those gathered around:

> Come hold him by the head,
> Children, come hold him by the feet.
> Let the kin of the dead come and hold him by the head.[2]

Bearing her alabaster jar of burial oils, his mother comes forward to anoint his head and feet. As the sacred oils touch him, he becomes aware of a powerful wave of light that shines into his soul and reveals all the thoughts and memories of his lifetime, even the dreams of paintings he was never able to realize. He finds that he can see all the way back into the dim distances; he experiences all the memories, songs, dreams and thoughts of those who went before him—from the forest kingdom of Dahomey to the westward-bound slave ships, to the sugar plantations of Haiti, and to the often unwelcoming new land where he and his mother were born.

All that had previously been hidden is now revealed. When his mother whispers the secret name she had long ago chosen for him, she reveals all the other secrets she had previously hidden from him. From beyond the edge of the forest steps a man heretofore shrouded in mystery, but whom Victor recognizes at once. As Victor rises to take the hand of his father and embrace his mother, he becomes one with the wave of light that now envelops him in joy, love, and reconciliation. His spirit is with the vodun, and Victor Chambers knows that he, too, will be remembered and revered by those who come after him.

N O T E S

Preface

1. Victor Chambers's punctuation has been edited for clarity. The hand-written letters are reproduced on pp. xviii–xxxiv.

2. For a discussion and two different transcriptions of Sojourner Truth's famous speech to an 1851 Woman's Rights Convention in Akron, Ohio, see the Schomburg Library edition of Olive Gilbert, comp., *Narrative of Sojourner Truth: A Bondswoman of Olden Time, With a History of Her Labors and Correspondence Drawn from Her "Book of Life"*, introduction by Jeffrey C. Stewart (New York and Oxford: Oxford University Press, 1991), pp. xxxiii–xxxvi and 133–35.

3. John Blassingame, ed., preface to *Slave Testimony: Two Centuries of Letters, Speeches, Interviews and Autobiographies* (Baton Rouge: Louisiana State University Press, 1977), xlix–l.

4. Leon F. Litwack, *Been in the Storm So Long: The Aftermath of Slavery* (New York: Vintage Books, 1979), xiii.

Chapter 1

1. Gary B. Nash, "Reverberations of Haiti in North America: Black Saint Domingans in Philadelphia," *Pennsylvania History* 65 (Supplement, 1998): 45–53.

2. Nash, "Reverberations of Haiti," 67.

3. Melville J. Herskovitz, *Dahomey, An Ancient West African Kingdom* (Evanston, Ill.: Northwestern University Press, 1867), 194–209.

4. Ibid., 259.

5. Ibid., 149, 151, 370.

6. Thomas Ott, *The Haitian Revolution, 1789–1804* (Knoxville: University of Tennessee Press, 1967), 16–17.

7. Robin Blackburn, *The Overthrow of Colonial Slavery, 1776–1848* (New York: Verso, 1988), 191.

8. T. Lothrup Stoddard, *The French Revolution in San Domingo* (New York: Houghton Mifflin, 1914), 60.

9. Herbert Klein, *The Middle Passage: Comparative Studies in the African Slave Trade* (Princeton: Princeton University Press, 1998), 78.

10. Ott, *The Haitian Revolution*, 46.

11. Ibid., 47–48.

12. Blackburn, *The Overthrow of Colonial Slavery*, 191.

13. Laws for the Commonwealth of Pennsylvania. 2, 492.

14. Gary B. Nash, *Forging Freedom: The Formation of Philadelphia's Black Community 1720–1840* (Cambridge: Harvard University Press, 1991), 62–65.

Chapter 2

1. J. H. Powell, *Bring Out Your Dead: The Great Plague of Yellow Fever in Philadelphia in 1793* (Philadelphia: University of Pennsylvania Press, 1947), 8–63.

2. *Le Courier Politique*, December 19, 1793.

3. Powell, *Bring Out Your Dead*, 8–63.

4. Nash, *Forging Freedom*, 121–25.

5. Powell, *Bring Out Your Dead*, 90–113.

6. Harry Emerson Wildes, *Lonely Midas: The Story of Stephen Girard* (New York: Farrar & Rinehart, 1943), 119.

7. Nash, *Forging Freedom*, 127.

8. Nash, "Reverberations of Haiti in North America," 51–55.

9. Allen Ballard, *One More Day's Journey: The Story of a Family and a People* (New York: McGraw-Hill, 1984), 30.

10. Carl W. Bolivar, "Pencil Pusher Points" column, *Philadelphia Tribune*, March 1913.

11. Victor Chambers obituary, *Providence Chronicle*, January 1, 1944, 8.

12. Frances Childs, *French Refugee Life in the United States, 1790–1800* (Baltimore: The Johns Hopkins University Press, 1940), 62–84.

13. W. E. B. DuBois, *The Philadelphia Negro: A Social Study* (Philadelphia: University of Pennsylvania Press, 1996), 141–42.

14. Ibid.

15. Mayor Watson's correspondence, *The African Observer*, May 1827.

16. Harold Hancock, "Delaware in the 1830s," *Civil War History* 4 (December 1968): 320–31.

17. M. Sammy Miller, "Patty Cannon: Murderer and Kidnapper of Free Blacks," *Maryland Historical Magazine* (Autumn 1977): 419–23.

18. William Still, *The Underground Railroad. A Record of Facts, Authentic Narratives, Letters, etc.* (Philadelphia, 1872; reprint, Chicago: Johnson Publishing, 1970), 606–612.

Chapter 3

1. Edmond S. Morgan, *American Slavery–American Freedom: The Ordeal of Colonial Virginia* (New York: W.W. Norton, 1975), 314.

2. Cited in ibid., 312.

3. Ibid., 313.

4. C. Vann Woodward, ed., *Mary Chesnut's Civil War* (New Haven: Yale University Press, 1981), 102.

5. Ina Chang, *A Separate Battle. Women and the Civil War* (New York: Puffin Press, 1996), 14.

6. Walter H. Mazy, *George Washington and the Negro* (Washington, D.C.: Associated Publishers, 1932), 92–95.

7. Thomas Jefferson, *Notes on the State of Virginia* (Baltimore: W. Pechin, 1800); edited with an introduction and notes by William H. Peden (Chapel Hill: University of North Carolina Press, for the Institute of Early American History and Culture, Williamsburg, Va., 1954; repr. New York: Norton, 1972), 137–45.

8. Frederick Bancroft, *Slave Trading in the Old South* (Baltimore: J. H. Furst, 1931), 322.

9. John W. Blassingame, ed., *Slave Testimony: Two Centuries of Letters, Speeches, Interviews and Autobiographies* (Baton Rouge: Louisiana State University Press, 1977), 343.

10. Ibid., 705.

Chapter 4

1. Pocahontas Wight Edmunds, compiler, *History of Halifax County* (Halifax, Va.: privately printed, 1978), 1:76.

2. Bancroft, *Slave Trading in the Old South*, 91.

3. Ibid., 285–86.

4. Wirt Johnson Carrington, *A History of Halifax County, Virginia* (Baltimore: Regional Publishing, 1969), 189.

5. Ibid.

140   NOTES TO PP. 35-49

6. John A. Barksdale, *A Barksdale Family History and Genealogy* (Richmond, Va., 1940), section 14, 351.

7. Ibid., 352–53.

8. Ibid.

9. Ibid., 353.

10. Ibid, 354, 356.

11. Philip Pregill and Nancy Volkman, *Landscapes in History* (New York: Van Nostrand Reinhold, 1993), 202.

12. "Brooklyn: Home of Elizabeth and Ruth Barksdale," Works Progress Administration of Virginia Historical Inventory, no. 45, June 25, 1937, 43–44.

13. Harry Pfanz, *Gettysburg: The Second Day* (Chapel Hill: University of North Carolina Press, 1987), 321.

Chapter 5

1. Blassingame, *Slave Testimony*, 338.

2. Henry Louis Gates Jr., ed., *Six Women's Slave Narratives*, Schomburg Library of Nineteenth-Century Black Women Writers (New York: Oxford University Press, 1988), 4–5.

3. Wilma King, *Stolen Childhood: Slave Youth in Nineteenth-Century America* (Bloomington: Indiana University Press, 1915), 62.

4. Blassingame, *Slave Testimony*, 447.

5. Booker T. Washington, *Up From Slavery* (New York: Gramercy Books, 1993),

6. Ibid., 4–5.

7. Charles Perdue et al., *Weevils in the Wheat: Interviews with Virginia Ex-Slaves* (Charlottesville: University of Virginia Press, 1976), 322.

8. King, *Stolen Childhood*, 96.

9. Ibid., 113.

10. Francis Earle Lutz, *The Prince George-Hopewell Story* (Richmond: William Byrd Press, 1957), 142.

11. Todd L. Savitt, *Medicine and Slavery: The Diseases and Care of Blacks in Antebellum Virginia* (Urbana: University of Illinois Press, 1978), 186.

12. Ibid., 122–28.

13. Washington, *Up from Slavery*, 6.

14. Blassingame, *Slave Testimony*, 343.

15. John W. Blassingame, *The Slave Community: Plantation Life in the Antebellum South* (New York: Oxford University Press, 1972), 214.

16. Frederick Douglass, *My Bondage and My Freedom* (New York: Arno Press, 1968), 279.

17. Ira Berlin, *Slaves Without Masters, The Free Negro in the Antebellum South* (New York: New Press, 1974), 70–81.

18. Ibid., 300.

19. Reverend Harry R. Mathis, ed., *Along the Border: A History of Virgilina; The Surrounding Counties of Halifax and Mecklenburg in Virginia, and Parson and Granville Counties in North Carolina* (Oxford, N.C.: Coble Press, 1964), 68.

20. Eli Shepard, *Plantation Songs* (New York: R. H. Russel, 1901), 131.

21. Lutz, *The Prince George-Hopewell Story*, 129.

22. Douglass, *My Bondage and My Freedom*, 186.

23. Herskovitz, *Dahomey*, 374.

24. National Aeronautics and Space Administration, Space Science News web page Science@NASA: "Early Birds Catch the Leonids," <http://science.nasa.gov/newhome/headlines/ast19nov98_1.htm>.

Chapter 6

1. Blassingame, *Slave Testimony*, 221.

2. Ibid., 220.

3. Ibid., 221.

4. Elizabeth Fox-Genovese, "Strategies and Forms of Resistance: Focus on Slave Women," *Resistance Studies in African, Caribbean and Afro-American History* (Amherst: University of Massachusetts Press), 143.

5. Edwin Morris Betts, ed., *Jefferson's Farm Book, with Commentary and Relevant Extracts from Other Writings* (published for the American Philosophical Society by Princeton University Press, 1953), part 2, 46.

6. Frederick Law Olmstead, *The Cotton Kingdom: A Traveler's Observation on Slavery in the American Slave States* (New York, 1953), 181.

7. Blassingame, *Slave Testimony*, 49.

8. Mary Boykin Chesnut, *A Diary from Dixie*, ed. Ben Ames Williams, foreword by Edmund Wilson (Boston: Houghton Mifflin, 1949; Cambridge: Harvard University Press, 1980), 87.

9. David L. Lewis, ed., *W. E. B. Du Bois: A Reader* (New York: Henry Holt, 1995), 304.

10. Litwack, *Been in the Storm*, 159.

11. Earl Conrad, *Harriet Tubman* (Washington, D.C.: Associated Publishers, 1943), 67.

12. Ira Berlin, *Many Thousands Gone: The First Two Centuries of Slavery in North America* (Cambridge: Harvard University Press, Belknap Press, 1998), p. 111.

13. 1833–1873 *Congressional Globe*, 36th Cong., 1st sess. 1672 (1860). Appendix, 170.

14. Washington, *Up from Slavery*, 16.

Chapter 7

1. Litwack, *Been in the Storm*, 52.

2. Bell Irvin Wiley, ed., *The Life of Billy Yank. The Common Soldier of the Union* (Indianapolis: Indiana University Press, 1943), 175.

3. Litwack, *Been in the Storm*, 56.

4. Ibid., 107.

5. Blassingame, *Slave Testimony*, 744.

6. Ibid., 688.

7. Charles Blockson, *The Underground Railroad* (New York: Prentice Hall Press, 1987), 98.

8. Douglass, *My Bondage and My Freedom*, 273

9. Still, *The Underground Railroad*, 50.

10. Blassingame, *Slave Testimony*, 543.

11. William S. McFeeley, *Frederick Douglass* (New York: W.W. Norton, 1991), 69–71.

12. Allen Pinkerton, *The Spy of the Rebellion. History of the Spy System of the United States Army During the Rebellion* (New York: Carleton Press, 1883), 27–58.

13. Alexander Ross, *Recollections and Experiences of an Abolitionist* (Toronto: Rowell and Hutchinson, 1875), 50–51.

14. Levi Coffin, *Reminiscences* (Cincinnati: Robert Clark, 1846), 254–56.

15. Savitt, *Medicine and Slavery*, 180–82.

16. Edwin B. Coddington, *The Gettysburg Campaign. A Study in Command* (New York: Simon and Schuster, 1997), 56.

17. Ibid.

18. Ibid., 61.

19. U. S. War Department, *The War of the Rebellion: A Compilation of the Official Records of the Union and Confederate Armies* (Washington, D.C.: United States Government Printing Office, 1880–1901), 128 vols., 27 (3):118 and 147. Hereafter cited as *OR*.

20. Conrad, *Tubman*, 297.

Chapter 8

1. Charles L. Blockson, *Hippocrene Guide to the Underground Railroad* (New York: Hippocrene Books, 1994), 114.

2. Theodore McAllister, "The McAllister Mill. An 'Underground' Station Where the Battle of Gettysburg Was Fought," *The Miller's Review* 6 (March 15, 1912): 206.

3. 1860 Federal Census for Adams County, Pennsylvania. Adams County Historical Society Archives, Gettysburg, Pa.

4. Blockson, *Hippocrene Guide to the Underground Railroad*, 114. See also Palm Family Papers, file 100, Adams County Historical Society, Gettysburg, Pa.

5. Basil Biggs Obituary, *Gettysburg Compiler*, June 13, 1906.

6. Quoted in Jacob Hoke, *The Great Invasion of 1863, or, General Lee in Pennsylvania* (Dayton, Ohio, Otterbein Press, 1913), 95–96.

7. *OR*, 27 (3): 369.

8. W. P. Conrad and Ted Alexander, *When War Passed This Way* (Greencastle: Greencastle Bicentennial Publication, 1982), 137.

9. Tillie (Pierce) Alleman, *At Gettysburg, or What a Girl Heard and Saw on the Battlefield* (New York: Lake Borland, 1889), 19.

10. Catherine Mary White Foster, "The Story of the Battle: Some of the Things the People of the Town Went Through," *Gettysburg Compiler*, June 24, 1904.

11. Clifton Johnson, *Battlefield Adventures* (Boston: Houghton Mifflin, 1915), 192.

12. Henry E. Jacobs, "Meteorology of the Battle," *Gettysburg Star and Sentinel*, 11 August 1885.

13. William Bayly, "Personal Stories of the Battle," *Gettysburg Compiler*, October 1888.

14. Major Joseph C. Rosengarter, speech delivered at the unveiling of the equestrian statue in honor of Major General John Fulton Reynolds, Gettysburg, Pa., July 1, 1899. Reprinted in *Ceremonies at the Dedication of the Monuments Erected by the Commonwealth of Pennsylvania to Major General George C. Meade, Major General Winfield S. Hancock, and Major General John F. Reynolds* (Harrisburg, Pa.: printed for the Pennsylvania State Archives, 1904), 96, 97.

15. Lieutenant Frank A. Haskell and Colonel William C. Oates, *Gettysburg* (New York: Bantam Books, 1992), 151.

16. Remarks of Brevet Major General Joshua L. Chamberlain, at the unveiling of the equestrian statue of Major General John Fulton Reynolds, Gettysburg, Pa., Saturday, July 1, 1899. Reprinted in *Ceremonies at the Dedication*, 93–95.

17. *OR*, 27 (1): 354.

18. Ibid., 354.

19. Obituary of General W. Dudley, *Gettysburg Compiler*, December 22, 1909.

20. Robert D. Hoffsomer, ed., "Sergeant Charles Veil's Memoir: On the Death of Reynolds," *Civil War Times Illustrated* 21 (June 1982): 20.

21. Ibid., 22.

22. Augustus Buell, *The Cannoneer; Recollections of Service in the Army of the Potomac* (Washington, D.C.: National Tribune, 1890), 59.

23. Richard Wheeler, *Witness to Gettysburg* (New York: Harper and Row, 1987), 145–46.

Chapter 9

1. "Man Who Nursed Officers in Thick of Civil War, Dead," *Providence Evening Bulletin*, February 8, 1924, 4.

2. Ibid.

3. Douglas Freeman, *Lee's Lieutenants: A Study in Command*, 3 vols. (New York: Charles Scribner's Sons, 1949), 2:xxvii.

4. Obituary of Armstead Lewis, *Providence Evening Tribune and Sunday Telegram*, February 8, 1924, 2.

5. OR, 27 (2): 367.

6. Pfanz, *Gettysburg: The Second Day*, 164.

7. *OR*, 27 (1): 404.

8. Ibid., 405.

9. Barksdale, *Barksdale Family History*, 283–84.

10. See above, pp. 60–61, and chapter 6, n. 13.

11. David Parker to Ethelbert Barksdale, March 22, 1882, Barksdale Papers, Department of Archives and History, Jackson, Mississippi.

12. Barksdale, *Barksdale Family History*, 286.

13. J. S. McNeily, *Barksdale's Mississippi Brigade at Gettysburg* (Publications of the Mississippi Historical Society, 1914), 243.

14. Barksdale, *Barksdale Family History*, 286.

15. Ibid.

16. McNeily, *Barksdale's Mississippi Brigade*, 241.

17. Ibid., 240.

18. Pfanz, *Gettysburg. The Second Day*, 555.

19. J. Howard Wert, "Barksdale's Death," *Harrisburg (Pa.) Telegraph*, November 16, 1901.

20. Robert A. Cassidy, assistant to Surgeon T. Hamilton, 148th Pennsylvania Regiment, to Mrs. Narcissa Barksdale, June 13, 1866, *Mississippi Index*.

21. George Hillyer, "The Battle of Gettysburg: Address before the Walton County, Georgia, Confederate Veterans," *Walton (Ga.) Tribune*, August 2, 1904, 10.

22. Pfanz, *Gettysburg. The Second Day*, 435.

Chapter 10

1. *OR*, 27 (2): 355–56, 458–59.

2. Haskell and Oates, *Gettysburg*, 115.

3. Union army Lieutenant Jesse Bowman Young quoted in Richard

Wheeler, *Witness to Gettysburg* (New York: Harper and Row, 1987), 245.

4. Ibid., 249.

5. Edward J. Stackpole and Wilbur Nye, *The Battle of Gettysburg* (Mechanicsburg, Pa.: Stackpole Books, 1992), 112.

6. Alleman, *At Gettysburg*, 63.

7. *OR*, 27 (1): 28.

8. Lemuel Moss, *Annals of the United States Christian Commission* (Philadelphia: J. B. Lippincott, 1868), 385.

9. Fanny J. Buehler, "Recollections of the Rebel Invasion, and One Woman's Experience During the Battle of Gettysburg," *Gettysburg Star and Sentinel*, November 1896.

10. Gerard A. Patterson, *Debris of Battle: The Wounded of Gettysburg* (Mechanicsburg, Pa.: Stackpole Books, 1997), 23.

11. Cornelia Hancock, *South After Gettysburg: Letters of Cornelia Hancock from the Army of the Potomac, 1863–1865* (Philadelphia: University of Pennsylvania Press), 1937, 8.

12. Mary Cadwell Fisher, "Field Hospitals of Gettysburg," *Philadelphia Weekly Times*, December 23, 1882.

13. J. Howard Wert, "In the Hospitals of Gettysburg," *Gettysburg Star and Banner*, August 5, 1863.

14. Ibid.

15. Eliza W. Farnham to Mrs. Kirby, July 7, 1863. Reprinted as "Description of Scenes After the Battle of Gettysburg," *Santa Cruz (Calif.) Common Sense*, August 22, 1874.

Chapter 11

1. Blassingame, *Slave Testimony*, 144.

2. Blockson, *Hippocrene Guide to the Underground Railroad*, 118-20.

3. Blockson, *The Underground Railroad*, 235–36.

4. Still, *The Underground Railroad*, 343.

5. Blassingame, *Slave Testimony*, 150.

6. Harold Hancock, "Not Quite Men: The Free Negroes in Delaware in the 1830s," *Civil War History* 19 (December 1968): 321–31.

7. Blassingame, *Slave Testimony*, 284.

8. W. E. B. DuBois, *The Philadelphia Negro. A Social Study* (Philadelphia: University of Pennsylvania Press, 1996), 38.

9. Frederick Douglass, *The Life and Times of Frederick Douglass, Written by Himself* (Hartford: Park Publishing Company, 1881), 170.

10. Eunice Glassberg, "Work, Wages and The Cost of Living. Ethnic Differences and the Poverty Line," *Pennsylvania History* 46 (January 1979): 17–58.

11. Ibid., 52.

12. Edward Price, "School Segregation in 19th Century Pennsylvania," *Pennsylvania History* 43 (April 1976): 121–38.

13. Romare Bearden and Harry Henderson, *A History of African-American Artists from 1792 to the Present* (New York: Pantheon Books, 1993), 44.

14. Ibid., 43.

15. Ibid., 45.

Chapter 12

1. Douglass, *My Bondage and My Freedom*, 51–52.

2. Charles W. Heathcote, *History of Chester County, Pennsylvania* (West Chester, Pa.: H. F. Temple, 1926), 29.

3. Robert Bussel, "The Most Indispensable Man in His Community; African American Entrepreneurs in West Chester, Pennsylvania, 1865–1925," *Pennsylvania History* 51 (1984): 329.

4. Ibid., 333.

5. West Chester Bethel A.M.E. Church records, Chester County Historical Society, West Chester, Pa.

6. Roger Lane, *William Dorsey's Philadelphia and Ours: On the Past and Future of the Black City in America* (New York: Oxford University Press, 1991), 188–91.

7. Boyd's Chester County Directory, 1888–1889 (Washington, D.C.: Boyd's Directory Company), 28.

8. *West Chester (Pa.) Daily Local News*, March 23, 1872.

9. Ibid., July 26, 1879.

10. Ibid., December 4, 1877.

11. Ibid., October 15, 1890.

12. Ibid., December 28, 1888.

13. *West Chester (Pa.) Daily Republican*, January 6, 1894.

14. *West Chester (Pa.) Morning Republican*, January 25, 1897.

15. Ibid., August 31, 1897.

16. Obituary of Isaac Cole, *West Chester (Pa.) Daily Local News*, March 28, 1939.

17. *Boyd's Directory, 1888–1889*, 29.

18. Federal census, 1880, West Chester Borough, Chester County Archives and Records Services, West Chester, Pa.

19. Bussel, "The Most Indispensable Man in his Community," 342–43.

Chapter 13

1. Robert J. Cottrol, *The Afro-Yankees: Providence's Black Community in the*

Antebellum Era (Westport, Conn.: Greenwood Press, 1982), 30–32.

2. Ibid., 95.

3. John S. Gilkeson, Jr., *Middle-Class Providence, 1820–1940* (Princeton, N.J.: Princeton University Press, 1986), 179.

4. John H. Cady, *The Civic and Architectural Development of Providence, 1636–1950* (Providence, R.I.: Snow and Farnham, 1957), 199–200.

5. Cottrol, *The Afro-Yankees*, 56–64.

6. Ibid., 32, 60–61.

7. Obituary, Providence Evening Bulletin, April 28, 1923, 6, and "Funeral of James LeCount," *The Advance*, May 1923, 1.

8. Andrew J. Bell, *An Assessment of Life in Rhode Island as an African-American in the Era from 1918 to 1993* (New York: Vantage Press, 1997), 106–107.

9. *Manual with Rules and Orders for the use of the General Assembly of the State of Rhode Island, 1887–1888*, prepared by Edward D. McGuinness, Secretary of State (E. L. Freeman and Sons, Printers to the State), 256 and 290. See also Patrick T. Conley, *An Album of Rhode Island History, 1636–1986* (Norfolk, Va.: Donning, 1986), 129.

10. *Providence Daily Journal*, January 9, 1901.

11. Bearden and Henry, *A History of African-American Artists*, 43.

12. *Providence Daily Journal*, November 24, 1901.

13. Bell, *Life in Rhode Island*, 51.

14. Ibid., 52.

15. Obituary, *Evening Tribune and Sunday Telegram*, February 8, 1924.

16. Blassingame, *Slave Testimony*, 560, 562.

17. Herskovitz, *Dahomey*, 1:255.

18. Andrew J. Bell, telephone interview with author, March 1997.

19. Laura Meade Kirk, "Rhode Island's Uncommon Common-Law Laws," *Providence Journal*, June 23, 2002.

20. Cynthia Ross Meeks (descendant of Selena Lincoln's family), interviews with author, March 1999 (telephone), October 1999 (telephone), and October 2002 (in person).

21. Karen A. Davis, "Sculptor Went Overseas to Gain Recognition Here," *Providence Journal*, February 16, 1996, B-1.

22. Obituary, *Providence Evening Bulletin*, May 29, 1933, 1 and 5.

23. Cottrol, *The Afro-Yankees*, 95.

24. *The Rhode Island Historical* Cemeteries *Transcription Project Index*, 1997, Rhode Island Historical Society, 27, 60.

Epilogue

1. Herskovitz, *Dahomey*, 1:374.

2. Ibid., 375.

Books

Alleman, Tillie (Pierce). *At Gettysburg, or What a Girl Saw and Heard on the Battlefield*. New York: W. Lake Borland, 1889.

Ballard, Allen B. *One More Day's Journey: The Story of a Family and a People*. New York: McGraw-Hill, 1984.

Barksdale, Captain John Augustus. *Barksdale Family History and Genealogy*. Richmond: William Byrd Press, 1940.

Bancroft, Frederick. *Slave Trading in the Old South*. Baltimore: J. H. Furst, 1931.

Bearden, Romare, and Harry Henderson. *A History of African-American Artists from 1792 to the Present*. New York: Pantheon Books, 1993.

Bell, Andrew J., Jr. *An Assessment of Life in Rhode Island as an African-American in the Era from 1918 to 1993*. New York: Vantage Press, 1997.

Berlin, Ira. *Many Thousands Gone: The First Two Centuries of Slavery in North America*. Cambridge: Harvard University Press, Belknap Press, 1998.

———. *Slaves Without Masters: The Free Negro in the Antebellum South*. New York: New Press, 1974.

Betts, Edwin Morris, ed. *Thomas Jefferson's Farm Book, with Commentary and Relevant Extracts from Other Writings*. Published for the American Philosophical Society by Princeton University Press, 1953.

Blackburn, Robin. *The Overthrow of Colonial Slavery, 1776–1848*. New York: Verso, 1988.

Blackwell, Will H. *Poisonous and Medicinal Plants*. Englewood, N.J.: Prentice Hall, 1990.

Blassingame, John W. *The Slave Community: Plantation Life in the Antebellum South*. New York: Oxford University Press, 1972.

Blassingame, John W., ed. *Slave Testimony: Two Centuries of Letters, Speeches, Interviews and Autobiographies*. Baton Rouge: Louisiana State University Press, 1977.

Blockson, Charles L. *African Americans in Pennsylvania: A History and Guide*. Baltimore: Black Classic Press, 1994.

———. *Black Genealogy*. Baltimore: Black Classic Press, 1992.

———. *Damn Rare: The Memoirs of an African-American Bibliophile*. Tracy, Calif.: Quantum Leap Publishers, 1998.

———. *Hippocrene Guide to the Underground Railroad*. New York: Hippocrene Books, 1994.

———. *The Underground Railroad*. Englewood Cliffs, N.J.: Prentice Hall, 1987.

Bloom, Robert L. *A History of Adams County, Pennsylvania, 1700–1990*. Gettysburg, Pa.: Adams County Historical Society, 1992.

Bontemps, Arna, ed. *Great Slave Narratives*. Boston: Beacon Press, 1969.

Botkin, B. A. *A Treasury of Southern Folklore: Stories, Ballads, Traditions, and Folkways of the People of the South*. New York: Crown Publishers, 1949.

Brent, Linda. *Incidents in the Life of a Slave Woman*. Edited by L. Maria Child. Boston: American Tract Society, 1859. Reprint, New York: Harcourt Brace Jovanovich, 1973.

Brown, J. *The History and Present Condition of St. Domingo*. 2 vols. Philadelphia: W. Marshall, 1837. Boston: Weeks, Jordan, 1839.

Brown, William J. *The Life of William J. Brown, of Providence, Rhode Island, with Personal Recollections of Incidents in Rhode Island*. Providence, R.I.: Angell, 1883.

Bumbrey, John Nordlinger. *Guide to the Microfilm Publication of the Papers of the Pennsylvania Abolitionist Society*. Philadelphia: Historical Society of Pennsylvania, 1976.

Buell, Augustus. *The Cannoneer; Recollections of Service in the Army of the Potomac*. Washington, D.C.: National Tribune, 1890.

Bynum, Victoria E. *Unruly Women: The Politics of Social and Sexual Control in the Old South*. Chapel Hill: University of North Carolina Press, 1992.

Cady, John H. *The Civic and Architectural Development of Providence, 1636–1950*. Providence, R.I.: Snow and Farnham, 1957.

Calos, Mary M., Charlotte Easterling, and Ella Sue Rayburn. *Old City Point: The First Hundred Years*. Norfolk, Va.: Donning, 1983.

Campbell, Edward D. C., Jr., ed. *Before Freedom Came: American Life in the Antebellum South*. Charlottesville: Published for the Museum of the Confederacy by the University of Virginia Press, 1991.

Carrington, Wirt Johnson. *A History of Halifax County, Virginia*. Baltimore: Regional, 1969.

Catton, Bruce. *America Goes to War: The Civil War and Its Meaning in American Culture*. Hanover, N.H.: University Press of New England / Wesleyan University Press, 1958.

Chang, Ina. *A Separate Battle: Women and the Civil War*. New York: Puffin Books, 1996.

Child, Maria L. *Isaac T. Hopper, A True Life*. New York: Dodd, Mead, 1872.

Childs, Frances. *French Refugee Life in the United States, 1790–1800*. Baltimore: Johns Hopkins University Press, 1940.

Coco, Gregory A. *A Strange and Blighted Land—Gettysburg: The Aftermath of a Battle*. Gettysburg, Pa.: Thomas Publications, 1995.

———. *A Vast Sea of Misery: A History and Guide to the Union and Confederate Hospitals at Gettysburg, July 1–November 1863*. Gettysburg, Pa.: Thomas Publications, 1988.

Coddington, Edwin B. *The Gettysburg Campaign: A Study in Command*. New York: Simon and Schuster, 1997.

Coffin, Levi. *Reminiscences*. Cincinnati: Robert Clark, 1876.

Conley, Patrick T. *An Album of Rhode Island History, 1636–1986*. Norfolk, Va.: Donning, 1986.

Conrad, Earl. *Harriet Tubman*. Washington, D.C.: Associated Publishers, 1942.

Conrad, W. P., and Ted Alexander. *When War Passed This Way*. Greencastle, Pa.: Greencastle Bicentennial Publication, 1982.

Cottrol, Robert J. *The Afro-Yankees: Providence's Black Community in the Antebellum Era*. Westport, Conn.: Greenwood Press, 1982.

Cunningham, Noble E., Jr. *In Pursuit of Reason: The Life of Thomas Jefferson*. New York: Ballantine Books, 1987.

Dirr, Michael A. *A Manual of Woody Landscape Plants*. Champaign, Ill.: Stipes, 1990.

Doubleday, Abner. *Chancellorsville and Gettysburg*. New York: C. Scribner's Sons, 1882.

Douglass, Frederick. *The Life and Times of Frederick Douglass, Written by Himself*. Hartford, Conn.: Park Publishing, 1881.

———. *My Bondage and My Freedom*. New York: Miller, Orton and Milligan, 1855. New York: Arno Press, 1968.

Drew, Benjamin. *A North-Side View of Slavery: The Refugee, or, the Narratives of Fugitive Slaves in Canada*. Boston: J. P. Jewitt, 1856.

DuBois, W. E. B. *The Philadelphia Negro: A Social Study*. Philadelphia: Published for the University [of Pennsylvania], 1996.

———. *The Souls of Black Folk*. Philadelphia: University of Pennsylvania, 1903. Greenwich, Conn.: Fawcett, 1961.

Edmunds, Pocahontas Wight, comp. *History of Halifax County*. 2 vols. Halifax,

Va.: Privately printed, 1978.

Fastnacht, Mary Warren. *Memories of the Battle of Gettysburg, Year 1863*. New York: Princely Press, 1941.

Fick, Carolyn E. *The Making of Haiti: The Saint Domingue Revolution from Below*. Knoxville: University of Tennessee Press, 1990.

Fox-Genovese, Elizabeth. "Strategies and Forms of Resistance: Focus on Slave Women in the United States." In *Resistance: Studies in African, Caribbean and Afro-American History*, edited by Gary Y. Okiriho, 143–65. Amherst: University of Massachusetts Press, 1986.

Freeman, Douglas S. *Lee's Lieutenants: A Study in Command*. 3 vols. New York: Charles Scribner's Sons, 1949.

Fry, Gladys-Marie. *Night Riders in Black Folk History*. Knoxville: University of Tennessee Press, 1977.

Gaspar, David Barry, and Darlene Clark Hine. *More than Chattel: Black Women and Slavery in the Americas*. Bloomington: Indiana University Press, 1996.

Gates, Henry Louis, ed. *Six Women's Slave Narratives*. Schomburg Library of Nineteenth-Century Black Women Writers. New York: Oxford University Press, 1988.

Gilbert, Olive, comp. *Narrative of Sojourner Truth: A Bondswoman of Olden Time*. Boston: privately published, 1875.

Giles, Ted. *Patty Cannon: Woman of Mystery*. Easton, Md.: Easton Publishing, 1968.

Gilkeson, John S., Jr. *Middle Class Providence: 1820–1940*. Princeton, N.J.: Princeton University Press, 1986.

Guthrie, James M. *Camp-Fires of the Afro-American*. Philadelphia: Afro-American Publishing Company, 1899.

Hancock, Cornelia. *South After Gettysburg: Letters of Cornelia Hancock from the Army of the Potomac, 1863–1865*. Philadelphia: University of Pennsylvania Press, 1937.

Heathcote, Charles William. *History of Chester County, Pennsylvania*. West Chester, Pa.: H. F. Temple, 1926.

Herskovitz, Melville J. *Dahomey: An Ancient West African Kingdom*. 2 vols. Evanston, Ill.: Northwestern University Press, 1967.

Herskovitz, Melville J., and Frances S. Herskovitz. *Dahomean Narrative: A Cross-Cultural Analysis*. Evanston, Ill.: Northwestern University Press, 1958.

Hoke, Jacob. *The Great Invasion of 1863, or, General Lee in Pennsylvania*. Dayton, Ohio: Otterbein Press, 1913.

Jacobs, Harriet. *Incidents in the Life of a Slave Girl, Written by Herself, 1861*. Edited by L. Maria Childs. Boston, 1861. Edited by Jean Fagin Yellin. Cambridge: Harvard University Press, 1987.

Jefferson, Thomas. *Notes on the State of Virginia*. Baltimore: W. Pechin, 1800.

Jefferson, Thomas. *Notes on the State of Virginia*. Edited with an introduction and notes by William Peden. Chapel Hill: published for the Institute of Early American History and Culture, Williamsburg, Va., by the University of North Carolina Press, 1955. Repr. New York: Norton, 1972.

Johnson, Clifton. *Battlefield Adventures*. Boston: Houghton Mifflin, 1915.

King, Wilma. *Stolen Childhood: Slave Youth in Nineteenth-Century America*. Bloomington: Indiana University Press, 1995.

Kirk, William, ed. *A Modern City: Providence, Rhode Island*. Chicago: University of Chicago Press, 1909.

Klein, Herbert S. *The Middle Passage: Comparative Studies in the Atlantic Slave Trade*. Princeton, N.J.: Princeton University Press, 1998.

Kulikoff, Alan. *Tobacco and Slaves: The Development of Southern Culture in the Chesapeake*. Chapel Hill: University of North Carolina Press, 1986.

Lane, Roger. *William Dorsey's Philadelphia and Ours: On the Past and Future of the Black City in America*. New York: Oxford University Press, 1931.

Lewis, David Levering, ed. *W. E. B. DuBois: A Reader*. New York: Henry Holt, 1995.

Litwack, Leon F. *Been in the Storm So Long: The Aftermath of Slavery*. New York: Vintage Books, 1979.

Lutz, Francis Earle. *The Prince George-Hopewell Story*. Richmond, Va.: William Byrd Press, 1957.

Marion, John Francis, ed. *Within These Walls: A History of the Academy of Music of Philadelphia*. Philadelphia: Restoration Office, 1984.

Mathis, Reverend Harry R., ed. *Along the Border: A History of Virgilina: The Surrounding Counties of Halifax and Mecklenburg in Virginia and Parson and Granville Counties in North Carolina*. Oxford, N.C.: Coble Press, 1964.

Maximilien, Louis. *Le Voudou Haitien* [Haitian Voodoo]. Port au Prince, Haiti: Imprimerie de l'Etat, 1945.

Mazy, Walter H. *George Washington and the Negro*. Washington, D.C.: Associated Publishers, 1932.

McColley, Robert. *Slavery and Jeffersonian Virginia*. Urbana: University of Illinois Press, 1964.

McFeely, William S. *Frederick Douglass*. New York: W. W. Norton, 1991.

McNeily, J. S. *Barksdale's Mississippi Brigade at Gettysburg*. Jackson: Mississippi Historical Society, 1914.

Moreau de Saint-Méry, Médéric Louis Elie. *A Civilization that Perished: The Last Years of White Colonial Rule in Haiti*. Translated and edited by Ivor D. Spencer. Latham, Md.: University Press of America, 1985.

Moreau de St. Méry, Médéric Louis Elie. *Moreau de St. Méry's American Journey (1793–1798)*. Translated and edited by Kenneth Roberts and Anna M. Roberts. New York: Doubleday, 1947.

Morgan, Edmond S. *American Slavery, American Freedom: The Ordeal of Colonial*

Virginia. New York: W. W. Norton, 1975.

Morton, Patricia, ed. *Discovering the Women in Slavery*. Athens: University of Georgia Press, 1996.

Moss, Rev. Lemuel. *Annals of the United States Christian Commission*. Philadelphia: J. B. Lippincott, 1868.

Nash, Gary B. *Forging Freedom: The Formation of Philadelphia's Black Community 1720–1840*. Cambridge: Harvard University Press, 1991.

Nash, Gary B., and Jean R. Soderlund. *Freedom by Degrees: Emancipation in Pennsylvania and Its Aftermath*. New York: Oxford University Press, 1991.

Neres, Philip. *French-Speaking West Africa*. New York: Oxford University Press, 1962.

Nichols, Edmund J. *Toward Gettysburg: A Biography of General John F. Reynolds*. 1958. Reprint, Gaithersburg, Md.: Butternut, 1987.

Oates, William C., and Frank A. Haskell. *Gettysburg*. New York: Neale Publishing, 1905. New York: Bantam, 1992.

Olmsted, Frederick Law. *The Cotton Kingdom: A Traveller's Observation on Cotton and Slavery in the American Slave States*. New York: Mason Brothers, 1861. Reprint, New York: Alfred A. Knopf, 1953.

Ott, Thomas D. *The Haitian Revolution, 1789–1804*. Knoxville: University of Tennessee Press, 1973.

Patterson, Gerard A. *Debris of Battle: The Wounded at Gettysburg*. Mechanicsburg, Pa.: Stackpole Books, 1997.

Parsons, C. G., M.D. *Inside View of Slavery, or a Tour Among the Plantations*. Boston: John P. Jewett, 1855. Reprint, New York: Argosy-Antiquarian, 1969.

Perdue, Charles L., Jr., Thomas C. Barden, and Robert K. Phillips, eds. *Weevils in the Wheat: Interviews with Virginia Ex-Slaves*. Charlottesville: University of Virginia Press, 1976.

Pfanz, Harry W. *Gettysburg: The Second Day*. Chapel Hill: University of North Carolina Press, 1987.

Pinkerton, Allen. *The Spy of the Rebellion: History of the Spy System of the United States Army During the Rebellion*. New York: Carleton Press, 1883.

Powell, J. H. *Bring Out Your Dead: The Great Plague of Yellow Fever in Philadelphia in 1793*. Philadelphia: University of Pennsylvania Press, 1947.

Pregill, Philip, and Nancy Volkman. *Landscapes in History*. New York: Van Nostrand Reinhold, 1993.

Quarles, Benjamin. *The Negro in the Civil War*. Boston: Little, Brown, 1953.

Ross, Alexander M. *Recollections and Experiences of an Abolitionist*. Toronto: Rowell and Hutchinson, 1875.

Salvatore, Nick. *We All Got History: The Memory Books of Amos Webber*. New York: Vintage Books, 1977.

Savitt, Todd L. *Medicine and Slavery: The Diseases and Care of Blacks in*

Antebellum Virginia. Urbana: University of Illinois Press, 1978.

Schlesinger, Arthur, Sr. *New Viewpoints in American History*. New York: Macmillan, 1922.

Shaara, Michael. *The Killer Angels*. New York: Ballantine, 1974.

Shepard, Eli. *Plantation Songs*. New York: R. H. Russell, 1901.

Sherman, Joan R. *African-American Poetry: An Anthology, 1773–1927*. Mineola, N.Y.: Dover, 1997.

Stackpole, Edward J. *They Met at Gettysburg*. New York: Bonanza Books, 1956.

Stackpole, Edward J., and Wilbur Nye. *The Battle of Gettysburg*. Mechanicsburg, Pa.: Stackpole Books, 1998.

Stake, Virginia Ott. *John Brown in Chambersburg*. Chambersburg, Pa.: Franklin County Heritage, 1977.

Stein, Robert Louis. *The French Sugar Business in the Eighteenth Century*. Baton Rouge: Louisiana State University Press, 1988.

Still, William. *The Underground Railroad: A Record of Facts, Authentic Narratives, Letters, etc.* Philadelphia: People's Publishing, 1872. Reprint, Chicago: Johnson Publishing, 1970.

Stoddard, T. Lothrup. *The French Revolution in San Domingo*. New York: Houghton Mifflin, 1914.

Thayer, William M. *A Youth's History of the Rebellion*. New York: Thomas R. Knox, 1885.

Turner, Edward. *The Negro in Pennsylvania: Slavery, Servitude, Freedom*. New York: Arno Press, 1964.

U. S. Congress. *Congressional Globe*. Washington, D.C., 1833–1873.

U. S. War Department. *The War of the Rebellion: A Compilation of the Official Records of the Union and Confederate Armies*. 128 vols. Washington, D.C.: United States Government Printing Office, 1880–1901.

Warner, Ezra J. *Generals in Gray*. Baton Rouge: Louisiana State University Press, 1964.

Washington, Booker T. *Up From Slavery*. New York: Doubleday, Page, 1901. Reprint, New York: Gramercy Books, 1993.

Wiederkehr, Macrina. *The Song of the Seed: A Monastic Way of Tending the Soul*. San Francisco: HarperCollins, 1992.

Wiencek, Henry. *The Hairstons: An American Family in Black and White*. New York: St. Martin's Press, 1999.

Wildes, Harry Emerson. *Lonely Midas: The Story of Stephen Girard*. New York: Farrar and Rinehart, 1943.

Wiley, Bell Irvin, ed. *The Life of Billy Yank: The Common Soldier of the Union*. Indianapolis: Indiana University Press, 1943.

Winch, Julie. *Philadelphia's Black Elite: Activism, Accommodation and the Struggle for Autonomy*. Philadelphia: Temple University Press, 1988.

Wheeler, Richard. *Witness to Gettysburg*. New York: Harper and Row, 1987.

White, Deborah Gray. *Aren't I a Woman? Female Slaves in the South*. New York: W. W. Norton, 1985.

Whitfield, Theodore M. *Slavery Agitation in Virginia*. Baltimore: Johns Hopkins University Press, 1930.

Woodward, C. Vann, ed. *Mary Chesnut's Civil War*. New Haven, Conn.: Yale University Press, 1981.

Periodicals

Bayly, William Hamilton. "Personal Story of the Battle." *Gettysburg Compiler*, October 1888.

Blockson, Charles L. "Escape from Slavery: The Underground Railroad." *National Geographic* 166 (July 1984): 3–39.

Bolivar, Carl. "Pencil Pusher Points" (column). *Philadelphia Tribune*, March 9, 1912, and August 3, 1913.

Buehler, Fanny J. "Recollections of the Rebel Invasion, and One Woman's Experience During the Battle of Gettysburg." *Gettysburg Star and Sentinel*, November 1896.

Bryant, William C., ed. "A Yankee Soldier Looks at the Negro." *Civil War History* 7 (1961): 133–48.

Bussel, Robert. "The Most Indispensable Man in His Community; African-American Entrepreneurs in West Chester, Pennsylvania, 1865–1925." *Pennsylvania History* 51 (1984): 324–47.

Dutrieuille, William. "A Family History." *San Jose Mercury News*, June 10, 1999.

Foster, Catherine Mary (Wright). "The Story of the Battle: Some of the Things the People of the Town Went Through." *Gettysburg Compiler*, June 29, 1904.

Glassberg, Eunice. "Work, Wages and the Cost of Living. Ethnic Differences and the Poverty Line." *Pennsylvania History* 46 (January 1979): 17–58.

Hancock, Harold. "Not Quite Men: The Free Negroes in Delaware in the 1830's." *Civil War History* 19 (December 1968): 321–31.

Hillyer, George. "The Battle of Gettysburg: Address before the Walton County, Georgia, Confederate Veterans." *Walton (Ga.) Tribune*, August 2, 1904.

Hoffsomer, Robert D, ed. "Sergeant Charles Veil's Memoir: On the Death of Reynolds." *Civil War Times Illustrated* 21 (June 1982): 16–25.

Jacobs, Henry E. "Meteorology of the Battle." *Gettysburg Star and Sentinel*, August 1, 1885.

Kachun, Mitch. "Before the Eyes of All Nations: African-American Identity and Historical Memory at the Centennial Exposition of 1876." *Pennsylvania History* 65 (Summer 1998): 300–324.

"Kidnapping." *The African Observer* (Philadelphia) 1, no. 2 (Fifth Month, 1827): 37–48.

Le Courier Politique (Philadelphia), December 19, 1793.

McAllister, Theodore. "The McAllister Mill. An 'Underground' Station Where the Battle of Gettysburg was Fought." *The Miller's Review,* March 15, 1912.

McCreary, Albertus. "Gettysburg: A Boy's Experiences of the Battle." *Mc Clure's* 36 (July 1909): 243–53.

McLaws, General Lafayette. "The Battle of Gettysburg." *Philadelphia Weekly Press,* April 21, 1886.

Miller, M. Sammy. "Patty Cannon: Murderer and Kidnapper of Free Blacks: A Review of the Evidence." *Maryland Historical Magazine* 72 (Fall 1977): 419–23.

Morgan, Philip D., and Michael L. Nicholls. "Slaves in Piedmont, Virginia, 1720–1790." *William and Mary Quarterly* 46 (1989): 211–51.

Nash, Gary B. "Reverberations of Haiti in the American North: Black Saint Domingans in Philadelphia." *Pennsylvania History* 65 (Supplement, 1998): 44–73.

Price, Edward J. "School Segregation in 19th Century Pennsylvania." *Pennsylvania History* 43 (April 1976): 121–38.

Scranton, T. M. "The Barksdale Brigade." *Memphis Commercial Appeal*, July 24, 1924.

Wert, J. Howard. "In the Hospitals of Gettysburg." *Gettysburg Star and Banner,* August 1863.

———. "Little Stories of Gettysburg." *Harrisburg Telegraph,* July–August, 1863.

Primary Sources and Unpublished Works

"'Brooklyn,' Home of Elizabeth and Ruth Barksdale." Works Projects Administration of Virginia. Historical Inventory #45, June 25, 1937.

"Ceremonies at the Dedication of the Monuments at Gettysburg Erected by the Commonwealth of Pennsylvania to Major General George C. Meade, Major General Winfield S. Hancock, and Major General John F. Reynolds." Printed for the Pennsylvania State Archives, Harrisburg, Pa., 1904.

Court Records. Halifax County Clerk's Office, Halifax, Virginia. Deed Books 43, 55, and 73.

"Creative Survival: The Providence Black Community in the 19th Century." Catalogue produced for the "Creative Survival" exhibit, Rhode Island Black Heritage Society, Providence [ca. 1985].

Humphreys, B. G. "William Barksdale and Barksdale's Brigade." May 1, 1876. J. F. H. Claiborne Papers. Southern Historical Collection, University of North Carolina, Chapel Hill.

Jones, William H. "An Early Picture of the Philadelphia Negro in Business."

Address to the Philadelphia Branch of the Association for the Study of Negro Life and History, December 1938. Charles L. Blockson Afro-American Collection, Temple University, Philadelphia.

Laws for the Commonwealth of Pennsylvania. 1780 Act for the Gradual Abolition of Slavery. Vol. 2, 492–97. Philadelphia: John Bioren, 1810.

Papers of the Pennsylvania Abolitionist Society. Manumission Records, 4 vols. Library Company of Pennsylvania, Philadelphia.

Philadelphia Port Records. Captains' Reports to Health Officers. September 30, 1789–May 3, 1794. Pennsylvania State Archives, Harrisburg, Pa.

Records of the American Catholic Historical Society of Philadelphia. Marriage Registers at St. Joseph's Catholic Church, Philadelphia, December 1799 to December 1808.

Register of Trades of the Colored People in the City of Philadelphia and Districts. Philadelphia: Merrihew and Gunn, Printers, 1838.

"The Underground Railroad." Special Resource Study prepared by National Park Service, U.S. Department of the Interior. U.S. Government Printing Office, September 1995.